PETERSON'S

Plan for Getting into

Law School

William G. Weaver, J.D., Ph.D.

Peterson's
Thomson Learning™

Australia • Canada • Denmark • Japan • Mexico
New Zealand • Philippines • Puerto Rico • Singapore
Spain • United Kingdom • United States

Visit Peterson's Education Center on the Internet (World Wide Web) at www.petersons.com

Library of Congress Cataloging-in-Publication Data

Weaver, William G. (William Gaulbert), III.
    Game plan for getting into law school / by William G. Weaver.
       p. cm.
    ISBN 0-7689-0394-7
    1. Law schools—United States—Admission. 2. Law—Study and teaching—United
      States.
    3. Law—Vocational guidance—United States. I. Title
    KF285.W43 1999
    340'.071'173—dc21
                                              99-058761

Printed in Canada

10 9 8 7 6 5 4 3 2 1

Contents

I agreed to write this book for Peterson's for two reasons. First, I am familiar with Peterson's tradition for quality, thoroughness, and integrity, and it struck me as likely to be a pleasant experience working with such a publisher. Second, I was dismayed at the useless and dangerous information concerning law school education and the law school application process that is floating around in bookstores and on the Internet in published and informal form. Some books on the subject have useful things to say, but often, superfluous commentary and material obscure the good stuff. Much of what is said in these books is so qualified and hedged as to be virtually useless to the person looking for straight answers on the subject of law school application and admission. I am a direct person, and some of my colleagues will no doubt feel I have said the wrong things in a number of places in this book. Though the advice given in this book may be direct and unvarnished, it is not that way due to lack of reflection.

Peterson's goal was to provide a book that would give people information on which they could *act*. To that end, this book aims to be as concise as possible in dealing with major aspects of the law school application process and the first-year experience while also covering the subject comprehensively. The rest of this introduction considers issues and questions that are likely to arise early in the minds of those considering attending law school. First, a two-year planner is included to help the potential applicant with scheduling events in the process. Taking an organized approach to law school application is crucial, and the planner below should be your guide for meeting requirements and managing your time. Also built into the planner are items to help give you advantages in terms of time and preparedness. For example, if you follow the planner, you will have the Law School Admission Test (LSAT) and the Law School Data Assembly Service

Introduction

(LSDAS) requirements done by August 1 of the application year, and the whole application process will be finished by December 1. This means that your applications are in early and may get a better look and that you also have all of the information needed to put together effective applications *before* you have to start making school selections and filling out forms.

TWO-YEAR CALENDAR FOR GETTING INTO LAW SCHOOL

See your prelaw adviser as soon as you think you may be interested in attending law school.

Spring of Your Junior Year

- Collect the Law School Admission Council (LSAC) Law School Admission Test (LSAT) application from your prelaw adviser or request a copy directly from the Law School Admission Council, Box 2000, 661 Penn Street, Newtown, Pennsylvania 18940-0998 (telephone: 215-968-1001; TDD: 215-968-1128; fax: 215-968-1119; e-mail: lsacinfo@lsac.org; World Wide Web: http://www.lsac.org/).

- Register for the June LSAT. By taking the June administration, you gain three advantages. First, you will know both your GPA and your LSAT score before you decide where to apply. This allows you to make a more informed choice, helps you save money, and allows you to tailor some of your applications for specific schools (schools that you especially like but may be on the border of where you are able to gain admission). Knowing all of your crucial information up front allows you to "spin" your application more precisely through the means mentioned in various chapters of this book. Second, if anything goes wrong and you must cancel your test results or wish to retake the exam in October, you are no worse off than the vast majority of other candidates. Third, the June administration does not interfere with normal school time frames, so you are not dealing with both class work and the LSAT.

- Register with the LSDAS. Registration forms are found in the packet you received from your prelaw adviser or the LSAC.

- After the end of spring semester, begin preparation for the LSAT. Prepare intensely for at least four weeks prior to the examination.

- Begin identifying appropriate law schools based on your LSAT practice scores and your grade point average (GPA).

Summer after Junior Year

- Take the June LSAT.

- Receive your LSAT score (four to six weeks after test). The LSAC now has a call option that allows you to pay a small fee on a credit card and receive your score via telephone beginning on a specified date. This way you receive your score much more quickly than waiting for the mailed report. You should take advantage of this option. For good or for bad, the torture of waiting will be over, and the sooner you know your score the sooner you can begin planning your application strategy.

- Write to law schools for catalogs and admission materials (August).

- Begin receiving law school catalogs (September).

- Review law school choices in light of your LSAT score.

- Register for the October LSAT, if appropriate.

- If appropriate, request that official school transcripts be sent to the Law School Data Assembly Service from all higher education institutions you attended. It may be necessary, in light of your record, to wait until your fall grades in your senior year are recorded. See Chapter 1 for more information on this point.

See your prelaw adviser as soon as you think you may be interested in attending law school.

Fall of Senior Year

- Meet with your prelaw adviser to review selection of schools.

- Request letters of recommendation by September 1.

- Take the October LSAT, if appropriate.

- Prepare applications. Applications should be submitted well ahead of the deadlines. Shoot for having all of your applications submitted by December 1, though November 1 would be magnificent.

Spring of Senior Year

- If you have not received notification, call law schools to see if your applications are complete (February 1).

- Fill out required financial aid forms as soon as they become available. Do not wait for acceptance to law school to obtain and fill out these forms. The LSAC's *Financial Aid for Law School: A Preliminary Guide* puts this advice in succinct terms:

  > "Obtain the Free Application for Federal Student Aid (FAFSA) from your college or university financial aid office, from a law school to which you are applying, or at http://www.fafsa.ed.gov. FAFSA is a need-analysis tool developed by the U.S. Department of Education. As the name implies, there is no charge for the collection and processing of data or the delivery of financial aid through this form."

- When completing the FAFSA, you will designate the names and school codes of all law schools to which you are applying. Information on school codes is available from any law school financial aid office or at the U.S. Department of Education. This information is also available on line at http://www.ed.gov/BASISDB/TITLE4/search/SF.

- The FAFSA asks for information about your income, assets, and other financial resources. Be sure to answer "yes" to the question, "Will you be enrolled in a graduate or professional school for the upcoming year?" All graduate/professional students are considered independent of their parents for the federal loan programs.

IS THERE A LEGAL PERSONALITY?

The short answer to this question is "no." Lawyers come in as many different personality types as we find among the general population. What prompts the title question is usually an insufficient appreciation for the diversity of jobs and work available for people with law degrees. Many graduates of law school elect not to practice law, but, even for these people, their law degrees provide them with excellent resources to get good jobs. There are jobs in the legal profession and jobs that can be had with a law degree to fit just about any personality type.

There are jobs in the legal profession and jobs that can be had with a law degree to fit just about any personality type.

Perhaps a better question would be, "Is there a law school personality?" Since law school environments tend to remain relatively stable from school to school, and since there is a lot of uniformity in law school training, the answer to this question is "yes." Law school, perhaps to its discredit, rewards a certain type of student and discourages students who do not fit the mold. For example, aggressiveness is usually a trait that is rewarded in law school, while the passive, the quiet, the nonconfrontational, and the nonarguers are ignored or perhaps even punished. This sometimes results in inequities in the distribution of grades and rewards. For example, women and students of color are less likely than white men to be aggressive in the classroom. Lani Guenier, a respected professor of law at the University of Pennsylvania, along with several colleagues, undertook a survey of law student performance. One fact that surprised nearly everyone was that women, even though their overall admission numbers are identical to men's, were much less likely to grade onto law review, a highly prized accomplishment.

It seems that the classroom environment in law school, even at highly ranked and socially aware schools such as

Penn, is a bit retro in its treatment of students. This issue will be revisited at greater length when discussing what to expect in the first year in Chapter 7. Notice that "good" law students are those who emulate the kind of thinking possessed by their professors. Note also that most professors have rejected the profession they are training students to enter. Most law professors do not practice law. Theoretical skill is overly rewarded in law school, while practical skills and abilities go virtually untested.

Law training is largely disconnected from the legal profession. Clearly, it is crucial for lawyers to be good at many of the skills developed in law school, especially the abilities to write well and quickly, to reduce vast masses of unorganized material to useable items, and to generate legally acceptable theories in support of a proposition or propositions. But there are many other skills necessary to the successful practice of law that are untested and ignored by law schools. You must realize that law school is nothing like the practice of law. If you must, view law school as a necessary evil that must be confronted and completed before you reach your life goals. If law school is just this evil, then law professors are the devil's minions, and theory is their chief torment for students.

IS LAW WRONG FOR YOU?

This is an impossible question to answer; only you can make this determination for yourself. Law is not wrong for any personality type; nor do one's interests make one wrong for the law. For example, people trained in physics, engineering, opera, Latin, marine biology, and sculpting are all welcome in law school. Law is such a vast enterprise that virtually any area of expertise you have going into law school will be of use to you in your career. If law is wrong for you, it is purely for idiosyncratic reasons of taste and not because your interests do not match the law or you are not temperamentally suited to its study. One should be especially wary of this issue, since many students who thought they would just hate law school or be completely overwhelmed by the experience do very well and even end up loving both school and the practice of law.

In my opinion, the law degree is the best, most flexible degree that a U.S. citizen can have. Rather than canceling out your interests, it can focus and magnify your area of expertise by giving it appropriate contexts for its use. For example, an engineer with a law degree may specialize in personal injury through product failure, or a physicist may argue cases in patent. An artist may become an expert in intellectual property and the rights of creators of art.

Only you can determine if law is not the thing you should do. There are no categories of people unsuited for the law. I tend to go against common advice and wisdom by advising people who are unsure about what they want to do to go ahead and attend law school. In fact, in my opinion, if you do not know what you want to do, you can do much worse in trying to figure out a path in life than going to law school. Even if you do not wish to practice law after school is all over and done with, the opportunities available to you because of the law degree will almost always mean that you will recoup your financial investment on your education. Law school will throw so many different things at you that if you cannot figure out what to do with yourself after three years there, then you are a difficult person to please. Also, much of what shapes our lives is the result of chance, and law school is a great place for "chance" to happen.

For example, an El Paso judge, who started a practice twenty-five years ago after graduating from St. Mary's School of Law, struggled at first and was about to quit law when she joined the YWCA. She decided to volunteer at the local YWCA to do some good work and meet people. She immediately began to have women come to her for family law matters, and, eventually, she became a family law judge. That was decades ago, and she still bounces out of her house every morning to go to work. She would not trade her work in family law for anything. Not surprisingly, she is a great family law judge.

We tend to be good at what we love, or to love what we are good at. Do not go to law school or even your first job with your future fixed in your mind. Keep your ears open and be aware of all the opportunities that surround you in law school. Let me provide another example.

A Berkeley law graduate in El Paso mainly practiced in the areas of business and nonprofit law. A former associate in a couple of area law firms, he eventually opened a solo practice and did very well. He also loved to teach, and, for the past seven years, he has taught courses at my school, the University of Texas at El Paso (UTEP). This last legislative session, at the instigation and hard work of a group of local attorneys and elected officials, the state legislature in Texas approved $1 million for UTEP and the community of El Paso to set up a border legal studies center. This Berkeley law graduate applied for the program coordinator position for the center and won it, largely because of his law degree. Now he gets to teach, practice a bit of law, select and pay law student interns for various community organizations, and

Clearly, for many people, law school is wrong for them, but the law is not. Keep focused on the fact that law school is only three years, and what you do with it afterward is for the rest of your life. Many people who disliked law school love being attorneys.

engage in research for publication. My point is that the law degree, like almost no other, can give you entry to a myriad of jobs and opportunities.

Clearly, for many people, law school is wrong for them, but the law is not. Keep focused on the fact that law school is only three years, and what you do with it afterward is for the rest of your life. Many people who disliked law school love being attorneys.

WHAT IS LAW SCHOOL?

Law school is normally three years (six semesters) of full-time classes. More than 180 schools are accredited by the American Bar Association (ABA). Accreditation through this body is extremely demanding and requires a school to have minimum resources in areas such as faculty, materials, and classroom space. In addition, the ABA maintains close supervision over the curriculum requirements of accredited schools. These requirements are most stringent for first-year courses. Nowadays, it is absolutely crucial that you attend an ABA-accredited law school. In many jurisdictions, a law graduate's ability to practice law is severely limited if she has not taken her law degree from an ABA-accredited law school, and, in today's employment climate, it may be impossible for graduates of non–ABA-accredited schools to find a job in law.

Almost all ABA-accredited full-time law programs start in the fall semester. A few schools have programs directed at students who are members of underrepresented groups and nontraditional and provisional students that begin in the summer prior to the normal first-year fall session. Students in these programs frequently do not meet normal admission requirements and can prove in these courses that they can still excel in a law school environment. These programs, however, are extraordinary and not relevant for most law school applicants.

Some schools also allow students to attend full-time twelve months a year. The advantage of such a program is that students graduate in roughly two years and a few months, rather than in the normal three. The disadvantages, though, can be very serious. Such a program means that a student will not engage in summer employment, which is often crucial in obtaining a job offer. Without summer employment, students look less attractive to prospective law firms, and many job offers to law students come from the firms and institutions that the students work for in the summer. Obviously, if you have no summer employment, you will not receive these offers. Again, schools that offer twelve-month programs are few in number, and where these programs are offered, they are optional.

Another issue that sometimes arises is whether or not to pursue a law degree on a part-time basis. You should only go to law school part-time for one of several reasons. First, you cannot gain admission to a regular full-time program. Second, you are pursuing a law degree as an adjunct to your present career or you desire the degree to gain promotion within your present company. Third, exigent personal circumstances require you to attend part-time. One reason that is insufficient for attending law school part-time is that you wish to avoid going into school-loan debt. As is discussed in Chapter 6, school-loan debt should be a concern, but it is relatively far down the list of items that should drive your decision of where and under what circumstances to attend law school.

Take the plunge and go to school full-time. Your chances of getting offers from firms with good salaries are much improved if you do things the "usual" way and go to school full-time.

By going to school part-time, you cut yourself out of the opportunities associated with summer employment. Further, though perhaps unwarranted, there is still a stigma attached to part-time programs. If you are already a professional and you wish to have the law degree to enhance your opportunities with your present employer, then by all means pursue a part-time program of study. However, if you are seeking a career change or are just coming out of undergraduate school, go to a full-time program. Wanting to have money or limit school debt are shortsighted considerations in this matter. Take the plunge and go to school full-time. Your chances of getting offers from firms with good salaries are much improved if you do things the "usual" way and go to school full-time. In addition, part-time attendance can draw out the program to a very long duration and present more chances for you to get off track and simply not finish the degree.

WHAT DO YOU NEED IN ORDER TO APPLY TO LAW SCHOOL?

In order to apply to law school, the applicant must have a four-year degree from an accredited college or university. No particular undergraduate major or course of study is required, and law schools welcome applicants from the so-called "hard" sciences. Law schools mainly look for students who have taken a rigorous track in undergraduate school and who have demonstrated writing and critical-thinking abilities. No law-related courses at the undergraduate level are required in order to apply to law school. In fact, law school admission committees may even slightly devalue an applicant who has taken numerous law courses at the undergraduate level. For more on this point, see Chapter 1.

Other than a degree, you need a valid LSAT score, letters of recommendation, a personal statement, and, sometimes, dean certification forms (supplied in the school's application). These items will be discussed at length later.

HOW MUCH DOES IT COST TO APPLY TO LAW SCHOOL?

Registration for the LSAT is about $80, and Law School Data Assembly Service registration for a dozen or so schools is another couple of hundred dollars, including the LSDAS base fee (explanations of these services can be found in the application booklet, which is available from your prelaw adviser or on line). These expenses are just the beginning. If you intend to take a professionally administered preparation course for the LSAT, the fee can be up to $850 or more.

In addition, law schools charge application fees that can range from $20 to $80. If a person applies to a dozen law schools and takes a professional preparation course for the LSAT, the final bill for the law school application process could easily be over $2,000.

Some law schools waive fees for ethnic minority applicants under certain circumstances, and the LSAC gives test fee waivers and application fee waivers for participating schools when an applicant is in dire financial need. Talk to your prelaw adviser for information and to obtain fee waiver forms; however, the standard employed by the LSAC in these determinations is very high: inability to pay the fees. Notice that this is not a hardship standard; just because the application process will work a hardship on you or your family is insufficient reason to grant a fee waiver.

You may, however, approach individual schools asking each to waive its application fee. Make sure you supply proof of your financial condition, such as tax returns and earnings statements from work, information about dependents and debts, and so forth. Each school can make a decision on your case as it deems fit.

WILL LAW SCHOOL BE WORTH THE EFFORT AND EXPENSE?

From a financial perspective, it is almost a certainty that regardless of what you do after law school, you will recoup the expense incurred.

Again, this is a question that only each person can answer for himself or herself, and this answer cannot be known prior to attending law school. From a financial perspective, it is almost a certainty that regardless of what you do after law school, you will recoup the expense incurred. For example, I work for a modest salary in the political science department at the University of Texas at El Paso. Getting a tenure-track professorship position is extremely difficult in any area, and I am quite sure I would not have this job unless I also had a law degree to go along with my Ph.D. I love my university and my department, and I would not trade them for anything, but I would not be here except for my law degree. I chose not to practice law, but that does not mean my law degree is not important to me.

It is the same in business, consulting, government, and so forth. Your degree will open up opportunities for you that would not otherwise be available. My opinion is that the law degree is almost always worth the effort and expense. Again, there is no way to tell this in advance, and such a judgment must be left to each person. In every law class, there are a few people who decide to drop out after a few weeks. Often, their classmates will snicker and say things such as, "Why did they even show up?" However, one cannot know how distasteful or objectionable something may be until one experiences it. Also remember that law school is not law practice; you may love the practice of law and dislike law school or vice versa.

PRELAW ADVISEMENT

Applying for law school is a complicated and time-consuming effort that is best handled with professional advice. Prelaw advisers spend a lot of time staying sharp on their subject. They attend conferences and stay in touch with schools, deans, the Law School Admission Council, and other prelaw advisers. Students often have very strange and unhelpful beliefs about law school, the application process, and law practice. Much of what an adviser does is to dispel these beliefs and help the student rearrange her priorities to conform to the topography of the law school admission process.

One cannot emphasize too much the need for personal counseling from a professional prelaw adviser. Most four-year schools have at least one such adviser. If your school does not have a prelaw adviser or you have completed school and so are not affiliated with an institution, approach the adviser at the school nearest to you. Most advisers are happy to help not only students, but also people in the community who need advice in the application process. These statements about prelaw advising require a couple of caveats.

Occasionally, a faculty member is saddled with prelaw responsibilities but has no real interest or love for the work. If you sense this to be the case, move on to another adviser. If no other adviser is available in your area, then consider

Recently, commercial sites have sprung up on the Internet marketing the same sorts of services that prelaw advisers generally give away for free. You should avoid these for-pay services.

consulting a prelaw adviser over the Internet. If you send selected questions to an adviser at a school you have been affiliated with in the past, it is likely that the adviser will be happy to answer your questions. Be sure to supply sufficient information to allow the adviser to give you intelligent advice concerning your particular situation.

Recently, commercial sites have sprung up on the Internet marketing the same sorts of services that prelaw advisers generally give away for free. You should avoid these for-pay services. These services use both active and former prelaw advisers and are very expensive, sometimes running into hundreds of dollars. I am not against people making money from this expertise. After all, I was paid money to write this book. However, you should avoid these services for several reasons.

First, they charge far too much for services you can probably get for free at a nearby school. One site, for example, had a whole menu that ranged from "basic" service, for about $100, to unlimited online personal aid with the application process by a prelaw adviser, which ran to hundreds of dollars. Why pay money to consult on line when you can simply get in your car and talk to an expert face-to-face for free?

Second, these services seem to imply that they can do wonders with a poor or mediocre record. The truth is, there is little that any amount of advice can do for a bad record. Of course, there are strategies of presentation to be employed, and that is a lot of what this book dwells on, but there has to be something of worth there from the start. Advisers do not see their jobs as trying to get a "bad product" into law school. Those people who have dreadful records are often told to look to other professions. This is not to say anything about those individuals' intelligence or ability to succeed; many, perhaps most, highly successful people have either no degree or a less-than-stellar college record. These services seem to prey on the applicant's anxiety and uncertainty about whether or not enough has been done to get into the best law school possible. It is doubtful that these services can do any more for you, and perhaps provide a good deal less, than the old tried-and-true prelaw advisers you have available at area schools.

Finally, the law school application process is expensive enough without multiplying costs needlessly. If people start using these services in large numbers, future applicants will wrongly think they must also take advantage of these offerings, or they will be at a disadvantage relative to those who do use them.

INFORMATION RESOURCES

- Your prelaw adviser. This should be the first source you turn to for information.

- Law School Admission Council. The LSAC has a wealth of information, and, given sufficient time, it will answer your specific questions. Be aware, though; because of their role in the application and admission process, much of the information distributed by the LSAC is nebulous, highly qualified, or hopelessly neutral.

- The Peterson's law site has an excellent section on law schools. Here you can find information on prelaw matters, discussion groups about law school, arguments of all kinds about whether or not you should go to law school, and so forth (http://www.petersons. com/law).

- The Hieros Gamos site contains a lot of information on prelaw matters, courses, schools, student organizations, etc. (http://www.hg.org).

- A former colleague at the University of Richmond has put up a comprehensive and thoughtful Web site for students who are interested in law school. He no longer works at Richmond, but the site is still up (http://www.richmond.edu/~polisci/prelaw/).

What Law Schools Look For

Chapter 1

GPA AND LSAT SCORE

As hard as one may try to get law school admission commit-tees to look at the "whole" person applying for a position, a candidate's success or failure is most closely linked to two items: grade point average (GPA) and LSAT score. The LSAT is almost always given more weight in admission consideration than the candidate's GPA. The LSAC claims that the LSAT score, taken in conjunction with the GPA, is a fairly good indicator of how well prepared students are to undertake the study of law. This seems like an ironic situa-tion for a number of reasons, not the least of which is that applicants live or die by an exam that is designed to predict how the student will do in classes taught by a person who has more often than not rejected or never practiced in the profession she is preparing the student to enter.

In law school, it is primarily the faculty members who make admission decisions, and they are tightly bound in their decisions by the objective criteria of the LSAT and GPA. Faculty members, of course, wish to admit the best class possible. Although there are many conflicts about what constitutes "best," most faculty members believe that classes are better off when there is a mix of students from near and far and of different ages, ethnicities, backgrounds, and training. Faculty members do not wish to be driven solely by the numbers, but they also must worry about the prestige of their institution and of getting students who will have the abilities to master the complex material studied in law school. The administration can take a more or less heavy hand in influencing this process. The institution, as opposed to the faculty, is often more concerned with the quantifiable quality of entering classes. In other words, does the entering class represent the highest GPAs and LSAT scores that the school can reasonably be expected to attract? If the answer to this question is "no," then there may be difficulties. Many schools also keep their eyes on school rankings and feel constrained to put a class together based largely on the numbers, lest they fall behind their competitors in the rankings.

Other pressures come from alumni who like to see their schools as highly ranked and regarded as possible and take a dim view of anything that might jeopardize their school's reputation. Of course, alumni are the source of much of the endowment money for a law school, and their views are disregarded at the school's peril. Nevertheless, faculty members try to balance these competing forces to put together an equitable admission process and to make sure that each entering class represents a range of students.

This system may not be perfect, but we are stuck with it for the time being, so you need to learn how to make your application as attractive as possible. Even though your numbers pretty much dictate your acceptance or rejection at each school, there are ways of putting your record in a better light and explaining bad patches and anomalies in your GPA and LSAT score.

Even though your numbers pretty much dictate your acceptance or rejection at each school, there are ways of putting your record in a better light and explaining bad patches and anomalies in your GPA and LSAT score.

GPA

In some cases, GPA calculation is rather straightforward and does not involve interpretation or evaluation beyond the number presented. For example, if you attended school without a break at one institution, never changed your major, and had no disastrous semesters, with little fluctuation during your undergrad career, then there is not much to say to law schools about what perspective to employ when evaluating your GPA. These cases are rarer than one would imagine.

Many times, people change their majors, realizing a little late in the game that biology or philosophy is not for them. In the time before this realization, their grades suffered because they were miserable or did not have an aptitude for the subject. Similarly, many students go to school for a year or two, stop taking classes, and return after a hiatus of one to sometimes fifty years. Upon return, the student almost always does better than when she took the first crack at college. Sometimes students get ill and try to fight through the illness, thereby blowing a semester. Sometimes students have to work long hours to support themselves, are single parents, or have a close friend or relative who is sick, has died, or winds up in prison. There are many reasons for anomalies to appear in a student's grade record. Perhaps the most common reason is the freshman semester, during which many people pay more attention to parties than to their school work. Whatever the reason or reasons, it is the rare record that does not contain some sort of anomaly. You should always make an attempt to explain these anomalies in your application material.

Be Proactive

If your GPA contains anomalies, do not merely sit back and let the LSDAS calculate your numbers. Provide a rebuttal to the LSDAS—be proactive. After all, it is arguable that overall GPA at each institution is not the most fruitful way to evaluate a grade record for admission to law school.

Calculate your GPA in ways the LSDAS does not. For example, it is often the case that the last 60 units of your degree program represent a higher GPA than your first 30. (Remember, law school admission committees generally see only three years worth of grades because application is made in the fall of the senior year.) If this is the case, do the calculation and argue that the law schools you apply to should consider your later work as a better indicator of your ability. After all, upper-division courses are generally held to be more difficult than lower-division courses. Furthermore, most of the difficult writing and analysis associated with degree programs is almost always found in the upper-division courses. Explain the amount and kind of writing you had to do. Better yet, have a recommender explain this to the schools in a letter of recommendation.

If, on the other hand, your last 60 units are not as good as the first 30, you are probably better off remaining quiet than pointing out your GPA in the first units. Law schools are very sensitive to students who seem to do worse when the material is supposed to get harder. A student whose upper-division course grades are lower than her lower-division grades will make law schools wonder if the student has the ability to master complex material and difficult concepts. Frequently, students return to school after a substantial layoff. Invariably, these returning students do better than they did originally. It is important to point out the time lag to law schools and the heightened performance since returning to school. In other words, do not let your record just sit there; slice it in different ways to make your package more attractive and to provide you with a more persuasive case for admission. The mere fact that you are attempting such a thing may make your overall package appear more favorable, as it shows you to be a person who is a fighter and a persuader—two characteristics that are very useful in a good attorney.

Insufficient Record

Another problem that plagues students in the admission process is that they simply have insufficient semesters to show law schools what their abilities are really like. Remember that usually law schools will have only three years worth of college grades in hand for the average candidate. Applications go out during the fall semester of the senior year, and, often, law schools make admission decisions without ever seeing a senior-year grade for many candidates.

If you partied your first year away and only slowly realized what you were doing to your GPA and your future during the second, it leaves you with only two semesters' worth of effort that represents you at your best. This is a weak limb on which to hang your chances for admission to law school, but it is a very common situation. There are several things you can do to help alleviate this problem.

First, you can wait to submit your transcript from your current school until the fall grades of your senior year have been officially posted by your school registrar. If you had a very good semester, it will give law schools another semester's worth of grades to look at in making their decisions. The drawback in doing this is that you have considerably delayed completion of your LSDAS file. In this event, the

If you partied your first year away and only slowly realized what you were doing to your GPA and your future during the second, it leaves you with only two semesters' worth of effort that represents you at your best. There are several things you can do to help alleviate this problem.

LSDAS will not be done processing your grades until probably late January or early February. This puts your application right in the middle of the squeeze time that you should avoid by having LSDAS material in by September 1 and law applications in by December 1 (see Chapter 2).

A second way of approaching the problem of an insufficient grade record is to double major. This is a decision that has serious consequences. Most notably, you will delay your graduation date by at least a year. On the other hand, it gives you opportunities in a new major while you are at your most mature and when you have mastered class and test preparation. If, after reading the material here and consulting with your adviser, you end up taking this option, make sure you do not graduate with your first degree and then come back for a second. The LSDAS utilizes undergraduate work for averaging your GPA only up to your first graduation. That is, if you *officially* graduate, the GPA for your second major will not be averaged in with your undergraduate work. Not graduating is really quite easy. Even if you have fulfilled all of the requirements for a given major, most schools require that you apply for graduation. If you do not apply, then you do not graduate.

There are three situations in which students should go ahead and add another major to their program. Before going further, though, there are several issues to confront. First, you must be very certain that you want to go to law school; otherwise you may be taking a course of action that does little actual good and costs significant time and money. Second, you should not be terribly concerned with extending your undergraduate work by at least an additional year. Sometimes older students are especially nervous about spending more time than absolutely necessary in undergraduate school. If you are going to be extremely nervous about extending your time as an undergraduate, then do not do it. All things considered, you should not be so worried about the time you will lose. After you go to law school, you will look back on your undergraduate days as a time of freedom. Do not be in such a hurry to work for the rest of your life (see Chapter 4).

If you are convinced that law school is the place for you, you do not mind the extra year or so in undergraduate school, and you find yourself in one of the following situations, you ought to consider double majoring. However, before you make any decision on this matter, you must speak to both your major academic adviser and your prelaw adviser.

When Should You Double Major?

First, on very rare occasions, a student will discover that she is in a major that is unacceptable for law school. Law schools, as will be discussed in the next main section of this chapter, are happy to accept pretty much any major. If you find yourself in the quintessential "basket weaving" major—a major that is completely devoid of serious writing requirements and analytical method—you are going to be in trouble when you apply to law school. Physical education majors, kinesiology majors, and so forth may also present the applicant with an admission problem. If you are a graduate of one of these programs and it is demanding in terms of writing requirements and analytical thinking, then you need to make that clear to the law schools. Supplying the schools with a brief description of the major requirements or having a recommender discuss the rigor of the program are two ways of handling this problem; however, beware that the burden of persuasion is on you; the evidence for the major must be convincing.

In addition, there are majors that, while acceptable in applying to law school, may be discounted for lack of rigor. These majors can vary, as law schools are sometimes familiar with the specifics of particular undergraduate schools. In general, education, criminal justice, and communications majors may spark a bit of doubt in the minds of law school admission personnel. This is especially true if you are applying to highly competitive programs. Majors and admission will be discussed further below.

A second situation that might call for considering a double major is if the extra work will significantly raise your overall GPA. After all, providing that you are in a rigorous major now, it does little good to take on another major and an extra year or so of school to simply wind up with the same GPA. Do the math; figure out what are the best grades you can make across the second major's curriculum and see how it will affect your overall GPA. Be honest with yourself; see what your GPA was in your current major when you could seriously devote yourself to school work, and then use those grades as a guide for what you might do in the second major.

> **If you find yourself in the quintessential "basket weaving" major—a major that is completely devoid of serious writing requirements and analytical method— you are going to be in trouble when you apply to law school.**

Obviously, some majors have traditional grading patterns that set them apart. For example, engineering students and others in the hard sciences have depressed GPAs when compared to the average liberal arts major. Law schools recognize this and take it into account, but you should be thoroughly familiar with the requirements, grading patterns, and faculty members you will encounter before embarking on a second major (or even a first major, for that matter).

A third situation where you may wish to consider double majoring is if you discover that you have limited talent for the major you are about to complete but have great talent with respect to another major. For example, a few years ago, a biology major came to me with a respectable GPA for the College of Science, around a 3.3. In her senior year, though, she took a course in Shakespeare and fell in love with not only Shakespeare, but also writing. As it turned out, she was a very good writer, much better than even the average English major. Shakespeare led her to become interested in law, and before her senior year was done, she decided to go to law school. I tentatively suggested that she double major, with English literature as her second major. She had never even thought of such a thing and seized on it right away. After another year of work, she had her biology and English degrees, with a 4.0 GPA in the English major. She went on to a very competitive law school and has done very well. If you find yourself muddling through a major that is not really to your liking, and you discover that your talent lies elsewhere, go ahead and consider changing your major or double majoring.

LSAT Scores

If you are lucky enough to have a grade record free of mischief and have a superior GPA, you are well positioned to apply to law school. However, a competent score on the Law School Admission Test is necessary for you to maintain that position. Let me say right off the bat that I think that the LSAT and the way law schools use it bars many students who would be perfectly fine or even brilliant attorneys. Nevertheless, we are stuck with the LSAT for the time being, and, even though few people can envision a law school admission process without the test, it is clear that many law schools are trying to make the test less determinative of admission than it now is. As it stands now, your LSAT score is the most important piece of information in your law school application.

However, it is important to point out that the test has numerous weaknesses and is an insufficient vehicle to depend upon to such a great extent.

What the LSAT Means

The LSAT is not an IQ test, nor should you feel a judgment has been made about your intelligence if you do not do well on the LSAT. After years of trying to predict applicant performance on the LSAT, I have given up.

In simple terms, there are two kinds of standardized tests to determine academic ability. The first type of exam focuses on what a person knows. Theoretically, a test taker can improve her scores on this type of exam by becoming more knowledgeable, by knowing more facts about the world, by understanding more chemical reactions, and so forth. The second type of exam does not test what you know; it tests how you think. The LSAT is an example of the second type of exam.

It is possible for a person who is terribly ignorant to do well on the LSAT. One can never have read a newspaper, contemplated Plato's *Republic,* or contributed anything at all to the community and still score in the 99th percentile of the LSAT.

It is possible for a person who is terribly ignorant to do well on the LSAT. One can never have read a newspaper, contemplated Plato's *Republic*, or contributed anything at all to the community and still score in the 99th percentile of the LSAT. It is not a general knowledge test or a test designed to discern personality types or strengths and weaknesses of character. The test is used to evaluate your abilities to solve certain types of logical problems in a specified period of time. The types of problems found in the LSAT are supposedly analogous to the types of problems you will encounter in law school and the practice of law. So the argument goes that your performance on the LSAT is a good predictor of your performance in law school. This turns out to be pretty much the case and is especially true if GPA and LSAT score are combined in the prediction. However, as indicated earlier, performance on the LSAT probably has little to do with a person's success in the practice of law, other than supporting the generally tautologous statement that the people with the highest LSAT scores go to the law schools that produce the students who receive the highest starting salaries.

The exam does a fairly decent job in predicting whether or not a particular student will be able to think like a law professor thinks, but that does not ensure that a person has the skills necessary to be an effective advocate for a client. After all, most law professors have rejected the profession for which they are preparing their students. A fair number of law professors are members of their state bars and handle cases, but many do not. A member of the faculty at my alma mater used to make it a point to show disgust with the practice of law in the classes he taught. He would say that he would never be a member of any bar and did little to hide his contempt for the future in store for most of his students.

Law professors should not confuse their choice of careers with the belief that law applicants should be screened for admission to allow in only those who can think like academics or are "inchoate" professors of law. Lawyers do much more than merely solve legal problems or come up with theories in law to aid a particular case. Sometimes, the only friend and supporter a client has will be her attorney. Lawyers need to be compassionate, caring, and committed, and no test can ferret out that information.

Lawyers also need good interpersonal, financial, counseling, communication, and political skills. What difference does it make if you have a degree from a premier law school if you cannot communicate with clients from a broad range of backgrounds and socioeconomic origins? It is up to law schools to make sure they include in their evaluations personal characteristics of the applicant along with quantitative measures based on LSAT score and GPA.

For the time being, let us bracket these complaints, and in Chapter 3, we will discuss how to handle low LSAT scores. Despite its flaws, the LSAT is the single most important piece of information in your application packet. Many schools will deny this, but their protests are belied by two things.

First, the index score (discussed later in this chapter) calculation formula schools use generally gives great weight to the LSAT score, even relative to the GPA. So your performance on a morning-long exam carries more weight in the admission process than three or more years of college work.

Second, the public relations literature of many schools gives prominent position to claims of their school's selectivity, based on average LSAT scores for their entering classes. Of course, attention is paid to GPA, but there is an uncomfortable feeling that often the school wants you to pay more attention to the LSAT information.

Make no mistake about it; even with a 4.0 GPA, a poor LSAT score can prevent you from being admitted to *any* law program. Conversely, a terrific LSAT can save you from a very poor GPA. Most professors would probably agree that GPA is less about intelligence and more about good work habits, motivation, and perseverance. If this is the case, then law schools sometimes reward the lazy, uninterested student with a good ability to solve certain kinds of problems but does not reward the person with a great work ethic, motivation, and perseverance when he cannot do well on a 4-hour test.

This claim is not overly dramatic. Several years ago, I had a student with about a 3.8 GPA. He was a wonderful

> **Even with a 4.0 GPA, a poor LSAT score can prevent you from being admitted to *any* law program. Conversely, a terrific LSAT can save you from a very poor GPA.**

writer and extremely dedicated to his studies. He also happened to be of Mexican-American ethnicity, and, therefore, he was probably given admission preference at many law schools. However, he also had a 138 on his LSAT, which put him in approximately the 12th percentile. His recommenders went way beyond normal restraint in praising his abilities, and he applied mostly to schools that were not regionally or nationally prominent. Nevertheless, he did not receive a single offer of admission. Now, take that same student and replace the 138 LSAT score with a score of 158, and he would be admitted to one of the law schools perennially ranked as the most competitive. To be more specific, if this hypothetical student applied to the following schools, he would be likely assured of admission to at least one (most likely more): Harvard, Columbia, the University of Chicago, the University of Virginia, the University of Michigan, Duke, and New York University. In stark terms, you see what the LSAT means to you and your chances of admission to law school.

On the other hand, if you have a 2.2 GPA, a generally disqualifying number for applicants to law school, an outstanding performance on the LSAT will virtually guarantee your admission to a good program. If a student with a 2.2 GPA scores a 170 on the LSAT, the 98th percentile, she can expect to be admitted to a number of law schools in the regionally competitive range. Obviously, you must prepare for the LSAT in a very serious and organized fashion.

To reiterate, you can do things to minimize the effects of a poor LSAT score, and these will be taken up in the next chapter. Bear in mind that convincing a law school admission committee to ignore a poor LSAT score is a difficult proposition, with even the best arguments probably receiving only mixed success from various law schools.

Index scores

Virtually all law schools utilize index scores. An index score is calculated for a law school through a formula supplied by the law school to the Law School Data Assembly Service. The index score is a function of GPA, LSAT score, and usually a constant of some sort. Notice, however, that index formulas used by the schools are generally skewed heavily in favor of the LSAT. This means that differences in LSAT score will have a much greater effect on the index score than will differences in GPA. So a student with a 2.75 GPA and 170 LSAT may have a higher (better) or similar index score at a particular school as a student with a 3.9 GPA and a 150 LSAT score.

The formulas used to calculate index scores for each school are available from the Law School Admission Service upon request. Of course, these index scores cannot take into account your extracurricular activities, motivation, integrity, or unique characteristics. The index score is mainly used to see how applicants rank based purely on the numbers. Remember that regardless of all the strategies discussed and employed and advice on how to make your application look better, it is this single number at each school that has the most influence over an admission decision.

You've Blown the LSAT. Now What?

Suppose that you score very poorly on the LSAT, say below a 144. If you are a nonfavored applicant, you are in trouble. There are still a number of things you can do, though you are going to have a very difficult time getting law schools to ignore your score. However, if you really wish to go to law school, you must take action.

First, talk to your recommenders and tell them that you have scores in the bottom X percentile of the LSAT and that your chances of being admitted to law school have diminished quite significantly. Ask your recommenders to frankly address the issue of whether or not your LSAT score is a good indicator of your ability to succeed in academic environments. Here you place yourself totally in the hands of the recommenders, for they may reach the conclusion that the score *is* a good indicator of your ability. It is crucial that you have a third party take up the issue because all of your claims, in your personal statement and elsewhere, that the score does not accurately reflect your ability will be dismissed as self-interested. Also, if you scored poorly on other standardized tests, such as the SAT, make sure that you give this information to your recommenders so they can use this as more ammunition to back up their arguments that your LSAT score does not accurately reflect your academic skills.

Second, carefully scrutinize your test. Add up how many correct and how many missed you had from each section. It may be that you lost a significant number of points in a single section. Calculate the average percentage correct of your other sections and apply that percentage to the section that hit you very hard. Then figure out what your score would have been had you scored your average percentage correct on the section at issue. Now you can report to the schools that you apply to that, except for one section on the LSAT, you would have had a 152, for example. This is not the most persuasive argument, but it is something, and suffering so seriously for a single poor section may make a few admission committee members think a bit. Of course, if you are fairly steady across sections, there is not much you can do on this matter.

Also, in order to engage in an analysis of your test performance, you must have taken a reported exam. Some LSAT exams are unreported, meaning you will only receive a score but no copy of the questions or your test sheet. Refer to LSAC literature or contact the LSAC to determine if your test is reported or not.

Finally, you obviously must change your application strategy to conform to your LSAT score. So focus on schools that weigh the LSAT less than do other schools. Also, look to schools that may be more flexible in their admission policies for one reason or another. New schools, for example, may be especially willing to entertain students with high GPAs but unimpressive LSAT scores. There are a number of very exciting and relatively new ABA–accredited law schools. Seattle University and Roger Williams are a couple of impressive young programs. The University of Nevada at Las Vegas, which is very young and will be out for full accreditation a few years down the line, is a school that seems to have excellent leadership and an exciting future. All of these schools are innovative, with seemingly high levels of commitment to students and facilities development.

New schools may be especially willing to entertain students with high GPAs but unimpressive LSAT scores. There are a number of very exciting and relatively new ABA–accredited law schools.

WHAT SHOULD YOU MAJOR IN?

Often, one of the most vexing decisions for a student who wishes to go to law school is what major to choose. Even after a major is selected, students often feel as if they need to take certain courses outside of their major that will help them gain admission to law school. Fortunately, unlike many other items discussed in this book, this problem is easily and readily solved. The answer is that, with a couple of caveats, you may major in any program of study you desire. Before selecting a major, a student should take a broad sampling of courses from various majors and decide to major in an area that she especially likes. You are much more likely to do well in something that you like. Remember, doing well and having a good GPA are the goals if you are really interested in going to law school.

The only rule for picking a major is that it must have a rigorous course of study. That can mean a significant amount of writing and problem solving, as in a philosophy major, or intensive methodological training, as in the engineering majors and life sciences. It should be said that simply staying inside your major and surrounding disciplines, while perfectly acceptable, is by no means optimal. Too often, political science majors, say, will fill out their curriculum of electives with courses in allied fields, such as history, literature, philosophy, and so forth. While there is nothing wrong with this, in the sense that it will not hurt you when applying to law school, it is perhaps a bit provincial and not the best use of your time.

If you are a liberal arts major, consider a minor in the sciences or taking mathematics through calculus. This suggestion will surely meet with resistance and rolling eyes, but the value of scientific and mathematical training is rarely adequately conveyed to liberal arts majors. Note that these courses of action involve risk. Do not decide to take math through calculus just because this book recommends it. As with picking a major, find things that you like and you think you will do well in. For one person, it may be math, while for another, it may be upper-division course work in geology or botany. The point is that the type of thinking taught in colleges of science is valuable to you in law school and in your life thereafter.

On the other hand, all that lawyers have are words; they have no other weapons on hand other than the ability to manipulate words. Many science majors get precious little

The scope of law is the scope of society, and people trained in virtually any area are welcome in law school.

training in writing and persuasion; therefore, the science major should also look to other colleges to fortify her ability to write. She should think about taking several upper-division courses in philosophy or literature and should attempt to insure that, in most semesters, she has one course that requires a substantial amount of writing. My law school, as do many others, divided the entering class into small sections—groups of approximately thirty-five students who stayed together for the entire first semester. We all sat together in our classes, and we had a small class that consisted of just our group. I was surprised to find that we had several engineers in our section, as well as a physics major or two and some people from life sciences. Law school is not merely for people majoring in the classic liberal arts programs. Law schools are happy to accept students from virtually any major.

Even majors that may seem a bit distant from what is done in law and by lawyers, such as music or Latin, are perfectly good vehicles from which to apply for law school. Often, the law requires the application of various disciplines to sets of facts to determine important features of a case. For example, political science does precious little to prepare the lawyer handling a case in design defect of a golf cart or structural failure of a building. An engineering or physics major, on the other hand, will have a decided advantage in understanding what needs to be done to further the case for the client. A person trained in the life sciences will better understand a patent infringement concerning a new type of rat specifically designed for research of certain diseases. The scope of law is the scope of society, and people trained in virtually any area are welcome in law school.

Nevertheless, there are some majors and course selections of which you should be wary. Certain majors are frequently discounted by law schools out of fear that they are not as rigorous as others. These majors include education, communications, kinesiology, physical education, some fine arts majors, and criminal justice. The flip side of this is that certain majors will be considered more competitive than normal. For example, engineering, sometimes English and philosophy, physics, and some life sciences majors may have their GPAs scaled higher in the minds of admission personnel.

On the other hand, even though many fine arts majors may have very rigorous requirements, law schools may wonder how much writing and problem solving the students actually undertook. In the other "less-competitive" majors, even though there may be a significant amount of required writing and problem solving, law schools are still skeptical of the level and intensity of training received. Indeed, part of the issue surrounding *Hopwood* v. *Texas* concerned the major of Cheryl Hopwood.

In *Hopwood*, the prestigious School of Law at the University of Texas at Austin was sued by students who were denied admission even though they had higher index scores than some minority students who were offered admission. They proceeded under the theory that discrimination based on race, even discrimination aimed at remedying the effects of past racial discrimination, violates the 14th Amendment guarantee of equal protection of the laws. They argued that discriminating against white applicants in favor of ethnic minority applicants is still discrimination. One of the interesting points that arose, among many others, is that the University of Texas at Austin discounted Ms. Hopwood's index score because she was an education major and so her GPA was held to be suspect. The law school believed her curriculum of courses was not as rigorous as those found in other majors. Ms. Hopwood's index score dictated that she be presumptively admitted—that is, admitted without closer inspection. Nevertheless "she was dropped into the discretionary zone for resident whites . . . because [the University of Texas at Austin School of Law] decided her educational background overstated the strength of her GPA."

In the appendixes, you will find excerpts from *Hopwood v. Texas*. The case provides wonderful insight into how admission works at law schools, since the process at Texas is similar to processes employed at other schools. So Cheryl Hopwood went from a for-sure admission to ultimately being denied admission merely because of her major. Hopwood and her fellow plaintiffs did win their suit, and the U.S. Supreme Court refused to hear the case on appeal. However, it would be naive to think that the sort of event that befell Ms. Hopwood does not occur all the time at law schools all over the country. After all, *Hopwood* is only law in the Fifth Circuit, which is composed of the states of Texas, Louisiana, and Mississippi. In the rest of the country, depending on what the law is in the particular circuits, law schools probably employ an admission process similar to that used by Texas prior to the *Hopwood* decision.

In addition, even though Ms. Hopwood ultimately prevailed, it is clear that it was not a violation of the law to reduce an applicant's index score because the applicant is in a particular major that is held to be less competitive than others. So if you are in a major mentioned above, you should ask yourself if you are in the major because you love the subject. If the answer is "yes," then go ahead and stay in the major and plan on taking some of the proactive steps mentioned below. If the answer is "no" or "uncertain," consider changing your major.

The fact is, sad or not, some majors can hurt you when you apply to law school.

Of course, this advice will upset the education, communication, fine arts, and criminal justice professors. However, the fact is, sad or not, some majors can hurt you when you apply to law school.

Suppose you find yourself in one of these majors, and you do not want to leave it. There are several things you should plan to do. First, ask your registrar for a cross-major GPA comparison. In other words, find out what the average GPA is for the various majors. If your major does not vary much from other majors in the liberal arts, then make sure that this fact is included with your applications. This way, the law school has no justification for discounting your major as less competitive if the average GPA of the students is roughly the same as other allied majors. If the registrar does not provide this information or will not give it out to students, have a professor or your department chair make the request.

Second, if your grades in your nonmajor courses are at the same GPA or better than your major courses, you can make the argument that you do just as well in nonmajor areas as in your major course of study.

Third, if you are required to minor in an area, pick a minor that is in a rigorous program. For example, any concerns about rigorous problem solving for a music major disappear when she selects a math minor and does well in it.

Fourth, ask around the department for students in the major that have attended law schools to which you are applying. Often, prelaw advisers track this information, and the LSAC actually distributes this information to prelaw advisers if they subscribe to this free service. Once you know this, find out how these students fared in these law schools. If they made it through all right, then you can point to previous law students at the target school who came from your department and did perfectly well. It would be great if a previous major from your department went on to be editor of the law review or some lesser post at one of the law schools in which you are most interested.

Sometimes, you may be able to use previous student performance at other law schools to convince a school that students from your major are well prepared for the study of law. For example, suppose you have applied to the University of Iowa School of Law and you are in a suspect major. Suppose further that in the recent past there have been no students from your department headed to Iowa law, but there have been a number that have gone to Northwestern, the University of Minnesota, the University of Texas at Austin, and so forth and have successfully negotiated these programs. Find those majors who went on to these schools with GPAs most near your own and point out the success of these students at very competitive schools.

Fifth, if your course curriculum requires extensive writing and problem solving not generally associated with your major, make sure that your application contains a copy of these requirements. For example, if you are in a fine arts major that requires a written thesis or a significant amount of written work, make sure to include a description of this requirement in your application and explain what your thesis or papers were about. Do not dance around the issue of your major; simply come out and say that you know that it may not be considered as rigorous as others, but that you are trying to make the best case for why you should be admitted in spite of this aspect of your application.

Another issue that frequently comes up is whether or not you should enroll in law courses offered in the undergraduate curriculum. Most schools offer courses in constitutional law, civil rights and liberties, philosophy of law, law and society, and business law. Be aware that you need not take any law-related courses in your undergraduate curriculum. Not only will law schools not hold this against you, they really do not want their entering students exposed to much law in the undergraduate curriculum. There are several reasons for this.

First, most law professors feel that one cannot learn anything useful about law in an undergraduate environment. Undergraduate professors usually do not have law degrees, often approach the subject from nonlaw angles, and cannot put the kind of pressure upon students to "remake" themselves in law as can be done in law schools.

Second, law professors do not like to get students with preconceived notions about the law. These notions are almost always incorrect or grossly skewed out of proportion to other areas of legal study. The last thing a professor wants in a first-year law school classroom is a student who thinks she knows something about what is happening.

Law school is like basic training for the mind. The idea is to saw everyone off at the same level and build them back up with a singular understanding of various concepts and principles. Some know-it-all in the mix does little to further anyone's education. Therefore, do not feel compelled to take law courses in undergraduate school. By all means, take such courses if you are interested in them, but do not take them merely because you think they will help you get into law school or will teach you something that will be valuable for you in law school once you are there. Undergraduate courses in the law are usually nothing like the courses you will encounter in law school.

Nevertheless, there is a move afoot among prelaw advisers to offer at least one undergraduate course that uses law school cases and materials text as the principle required

Law school is like basic training for the mind. The idea is to saw everyone off at the same level and build them back up with a singular understanding of various concepts and principles.

reading. This seems like a good idea, and in fact we do this in the Law School Preparation Institute at the University of Texas at El Paso. We use a cases-and-materials text on torts and run our classes basically through the same sort of stuff as found in first-year torts classes. Matters are not examined as deeply and intensely as in law school, but it is a good idea for all undergrads to be exposed to case law and how to read it.

In conclusion, major in anything you wish; just beware that certain majors will be considered less competitive than others. If you find yourself in a major that is considered less competitive than others, be prepared to undertake the courses of action described above. Do not just sit there—be proactive.

EXTRACURRICULAR ACTIVITIES

Extracurricular activities are important in gaining admission to law school but perhaps play less of a role than many students think. A misplaced concern with extracurricular activities can do a lot of harm, and there are several things to consider on this score.

First, do not undertake any charitable or service activities merely for the advantage they could give you when applying for law school. Service should come from the heart, and if you are not the kind of person to normally undertake such charitable work, then leave it alone. As with selecting a major, if you are doing something you do not like then you are going to make yourself and those around you suffer needlessly. Do not volunteer your time at the Little Sisters of Charity Orphanage if it is not in your personality to do so. There are many other ways to contribute to your community than merely the most obvious and charitable.

Second, make sure your GPA is in order before you go looking for organizations for which to volunteer. Do not let your GPA suffer because of your extracurricular activities. Take on extracurricular commitments in a slow, measured way and figure out how these new commitments are going to affect your ability to prepare for classes and examinations.

Third, if you are going to do charitable work, make sure you can clearly separate it from other activities in your life. For example, if you are a member of a Greek organization, make sure that if you list charitable work done under the organization's auspices that you are clear about the work that *you* actually did. Do not mention association with social fraternities as extracurricular activity unless you were a major officer in the organization. Affiliations, memberships, and so forth should be placed in the application proper, and almost every application has a space that allows you to list this information.

Fourth, think of how your commitment or extracurricular activity is going to affect the people around you, such as family, friends, and partners. If you neglect those closest to you, it can set the ground for personal crises that, in turn, can affect your school performance, which can ultimately interfere with or affect your application to law school.

Finally, note that it is usually easier to get into extracurricular activities than to get out of them. When you commit to an activity, make sure you are clear about how much time, money, and effort you will be expected to provide. Do not merely go down to an organization and say, "Here I am, put me to work." Make sure you are always in control of your time and do not commit to anything that makes you feel uncomfortable. Often, charitable organizations are desperate for competent volunteers, and you can find yourself being swept into many activities and situations you did not count on. ~~It is flattering in a way, since you are~~ being relied upon for so much. However, remember that extracurricular activities are an adjunct to your education, not its substitute.

Service Activities

Despite the snide things said about lawyers and the jokes aimed at them, it would be a safe wager that no profession comes close to rendering the amount of community service that is contributed by lawyers.

What sort of activities should you get involved in? Again, get involved in things you like. If that means working at the local chamber of commerce, then by all means do so. Returning affection and aid to a community can be done in a myriad of ways. Community service is also an integral feature of being a lawyer. Many states require that licensed attorneys engage in pro bono (free) services or contribute cash to attorneys who practice pro bono on a full-time basis.

Despite the snide things said about lawyers and the jokes aimed at them, it would be a safe wager that no profession comes close to rendering the amount of community service that is contributed by lawyers. Do not worry so much about how you will give service to the community; simply find a way that is enjoyable for you. In the admission process, impressive service, no matter where it is, will help your cause.

Nevertheless, purely altruistic undertakings probably carry more weight. If you have devoted a lot of time to the poor without remuneration, you are more favorably considered than the applicant who gave up weekends to help build a fraternity house. Again, though, only pursue those activities that come from your heart. The advantages you get from working in a soup kitchen as opposed to helping build a fraternity house are minimal compared to the suffering you will incur if you cannot stand doing that sort of thing.

One thing to consider is to get a letter from a supervisor or some other program officer detailing your work, the kind of person you are, and what your contribution means to the community. It does not hurt to add this kind of letter to your application, even if it is in addition to the maximum allowed number of letters (see Chapter 3).

Nonservice Activities

There are many activities that do not serve the community yet may be extremely important in your applications to law school. First, if you have done anything extremely unusual, you may wish to point this out on your application.

You may ask what counts as unusual. The only way to answer this question is to give actual examples. For example, if you have rowed from Florida to New York Harbor over the course of a summer, that is an unusual activity that you might want to mention and explain in an application. You might be a rock climber or a mountaineer who has climbed some of the highest peaks or the most difficult rock formations in the world. Perhaps you are a master pastry chef or make guitars as a hobby or play in a Mariachi band. Maybe you design rockets in your spare time, are an expert on the history and design of sunglasses, or constructed a homemade laser in your garage.

Often, students think that it is crazy to mention these accomplishments or skills in their applications to law schools. Actually, law schools like to hear about these sorts of things, because often, these things say a lot more about the person than can any other piece of information in the application. Sometimes there may be a little "weirdness rivalry" going on between law schools. Schools like to collect "oddities" or the unusual student. In these cases, the school may be saying to its competitors, "Hey, have you guys got one of *these?*" If you do have a unique hobby or have done something noteworthy, try to make sure this information makes it into the application proper. Sometimes, though, such a thing might be better as the center of your personal statement (see Chapter 3).

What if You Have Nothing to Say?

Extracurricular activities are nice, but it is troubling when schools place too much emphasis on them during the admission process. After all, some people simply do not have the time to engage in extracurricular activities. Many students have children, families, jobs, sick relatives to take care of, nephews and nieces to baby-sit, and so forth. If you did not have time in school for extracurricular activities, do not merely leave the record silent. Address the issue.

Perhaps in the extracurricular activities space on the application you might simply write something like, "I worked full-time for four years of school to pay my way through, and, therefore, had no time for extracurricular activities." After all, it is not right for a law school to punish people who had to work through school by favoring students whose parents paid for school and, therefore, allowed the student to have time for outside activities.

If you could not get involved in extracurricular activities, then say so. Even on this score, there may be more to say than you think. If you have been a parent while in school, you may have worked with the PTA, organized fund-raising breakfasts, or chaired or been a member on an ad hoc committee appointed by the school board. Also, there is no reason that providing day care for your relatives should not be considered a "community service." Look carefully at your life and what you do. Often, students are surprised at how much they really do have to say about themselves and their activities.

NONTRADITIONAL BACKGROUNDS

Law schools look to round out their classes with people who have had significant work experience or experiences not usually found in the average law student. These experiences are usually, though not always, a function of time, and so applicants in this category are older than the average member of the applicant pool by a fairly substantial amount.

Background experience that is highly prized in applicants includes military service, especially experience in combat or combat support; interesting employment history; single parenthood; the overcoming of poverty, an abusive home life, or a handicapping condition; and volunteer work in organizations such as Vista and the Peace Corps.

My best friend in law school was a Franciscan friar, and though he certainly had the numbers required for admission, his background did not hurt him a bit. On a related issue, sometimes older students are concerned that they will be entering a young person's profession and are hesitant to apply to law school. It is true that there are firms that may shy away from hiring an older applicant, thinking that she will not put in the 80-hour weeks they want to see. However, for every firm that avoids older applicants, there is probably a firm that welcomes the maturity level of older applicants and the fact that clients will not be wondering if this "youngster" can really handle their cases.

One thing is clear, no matter what firms do—law schools are very happy to have older applicants. In fact, being older, in and of itself, probably works in an applicant's favor.

One thing is clear, no matter what firms do—law schools are very happy to have older applicants. In fact, being older, in and of itself, probably works in an applicant's favor. If you have unusual background experiences, make sure you emphasize this information in your application and personal statement.

Of course, ethnicity is sometimes an important admission factor, and this matter will be discussed more thoroughly when we take up student diversity in Chapter 3.

The Law School Admission Test

The Law School Admission Test (LSAT) is required for application to all ABA–accredited law schools, as well as to some non–ABA schools. Normal administration of the Law School Admission Test occurs four times per year. Usually, administrations occur in October, December, February, and June. The June administration is given on a Monday afternoon. All of the other administrations are given on a Saturday morning.

People who belong to religions that observe the Sabbath on Saturdays may take the exam on the Monday immediately following the non-June regular administration of the exam. See the application materials or the Law School Admission Council (LSAC) Web site for further information on this matter and the scheduling of special administrations.

Each exam contains five sections and averages 125 total questions. There are three different question types, each designed to test different abilities. There is also a writing section, where the test taker must write an essay on a subject provided in the exam. Perhaps the exam plays too important a role in the admission process, but it is clear that the shortcomings of the exam are not due to lack of effort by the Law School Admission Council. Over the years, I have talked with a number of employees at the LSAC, and all of them seemed extremely dedicated and committed to providing high-quality service. Indeed, it is arguable that there is no standardized examination as vetted, worried over, and carefully controlled as the LSAT. Nevertheless the test shows a

Chapter 2

disparity of results for ethnic minority students and for students who are older than the average test taker. If there must be a standardized test used for admission to law school, then this is the one to use. Ultimately, it is the law schools that are responsible for how the test is used in the admission process.

The four-date testing tradition will probably be changing in the near future as electronic administration of the exam becomes feasible. For example, the Graduate Record Examinations (GRE) are now almost exclusively given electronically at numerous sites throughout the world. Candidates can sign up to take the test at their convenience and no longer need to wait for a universal exam date or the large rooms in which the exams are given. The Law School Admission Council is a very careful organization, and it is doubtful that we will see a rush to embrace purely electronic administration of the exam. When the changes start to come, there will probably be an extensive period of transition. Law schools tend to be very traditional, and we must remember that the Law School Admission Council serves the interest of its member schools. Of course, we must focus here on what the situation is now.

WHAT TO BE READY FOR

For many people, taking the LSAT is a horrible experience that they would not readily go through again. One strategy to help make it through the test and test preparation is to force yourself to love it. Of course, not everyone objects to the test. Some people even seem to enjoy the challenge of it all, and, with any luck, you will be such a person.

However, even students who love the challenge and throw themselves into LSAT preparation are still sometimes taken by surprise at certain events. Sometimes, students do not fully appreciate that actual test conditions are going to be substantially different than those surrounding test preparation. The first thing to be prepared for is that there are administrative events to get through before you sit down to the actual test. Remember to bring plenty of identification and your admission ticket and to arrive early. Make sure you leave your beeping watches, cell phones, and pagers at home.

The second thing to prepare for is that the room in which you take the test is probably going to be a lot bigger than what you are used to in taking the practice exams. A large room is going to be noisier, so be aware that the test will not be given in the silence you may have become accustomed to in your preparation.

Third, remember that you will not have four sections but five to complete when you take the actual LSAT. Students focused on their preparation often overlook the fact that they are going to be working intensely at solving problems for a substantially longer period of time than they are used to in practice. The extra section is used to validate questions for future examinations, but you will not be told which section is experimental, and there is no way to figure this out as you are taking the test; therefore, you must treat all sections as real sections. Notice that this extends the test by 35 minutes beyond what you are used to in practice.

> **Even students who love the challenge and throw themselves into LSAT preparation are still sometimes taken by surprise at certain events.**

SCHEDULING AND APPLYING

When to Take the LSAT

Make sure you read the application booklet carefully and that you apply to take the LSAT in a timely manner. You can register for the LSAT on line (http://www.lsac.org) or mail in the application included in the LSAT information booklet. You should take the June administration of the LSAT after your junior year. With the June administration, you do not have the sort of distractions you do with the other three administration dates.

First, you generally will not be in school during this administration, so you can devote your full concentration to the LSAT.

Second, you will have the most crucial information in hand—your LSAT score and your GPA—before you need to start formulating a final list of schools to which you will apply. This means that your list can be more accurate and your applications done earlier. If you take the October administration of the LSAT, you will not find out your score until around November 1 at the earliest, and that is only if you pay the fee to get your score over the telephone, as described in the Introduction. Because it is advisable to have your applications already submitted by December 1, you can see how time can become a problem. If you wait any longer to apply, you are going to be squeezed between school, the LSAT, figuring out a school list, and taking time to fill out applications. If you apply before you know your LSAT score, you are gambling that there will not be much of a disparity between your practice exam scores and your actual score. If there is a disparity of any proportion, you will have to adjust your application list and send out more applications. This means you have wasted a lot of time and a fair amount of money. Avoid all of this trouble by taking the June administration.

A third reason for taking the June exam is that if you need to cancel your score for any reason (see the section below) you can still take the October exam and be no worse off than the majority of applicants rushing to get things done. If, on the other hand, you must cancel an October exam the next available exam date will not be until December. Also, the chances that you will be able to really concentrate sufficiently to recover from a canceled exam score on an October administration are not very good, since most candidates will be consumed with papers and finals for classes.

Finally, you should know that the June exam differs from other administrations in a couple of ways. First, the exam is given in the afternoon, rather than the morning. This could be important to some people. If you are the kind of person who is charged up in the morning, but sort of flat later on, you may consider strategies for making sure you are at peak when the test is given. Second, the June administration always occurs on a Monday, rather than a Saturday.

Test Accommodation

If, for any reason, you are impaired in your reading or cognitive ability, or you have physical disabilities that prevent you from taking the exam under normal circumstances, you must contact the LSAC to discuss how the test can be modified to put you on a fair footing with the rest of the test takers.

If you suffer from a cognitive, visual, or physical impairment that hinders your ability to take the test under normal conditions, the testing service will, upon presentation of proper evidence, modify the exam to make it as fair as possible. Most often, the remedy is to either increase the amount of time allowed on each section or to provide the test on audio tape, in large print, or in Braille. On occasion, the LSAC will waive the LSAT for an applicant. If you think you may need a modified exam you must talk to the LSAC at a very early date.

Obviously, if you are to have extended time on each section, you will have to take a special administration of the exam. These things take time to arrange. The LSAC is very good about making things happen once they are satisfied that a true disability is present. The LSAC is understandably concerned about fraud in such matters, so make sure you have your evidence collected in a timely way. Have written statements from the doctor, neurosurgeon, or test center that diagnosed your disability. Make sure that the diagnoses are understandable to lay people and are very clear about your limitations.

You will need to fill out a packet of material supplied by the LSAC. To obtain this packet, or for further information concerning special accommodation for LSAT test takers, see the in-depth online help provided by the LSAC and click on the "accommodated testing" hot link. You can download the entire packet and information materials from this site. You may also call the LSAC at 215-968-1001 or fax them at 215-504-1420. People with hearing impairments can leave a message with Law Services via TDD at 215-968-1128. Finally, you can e-mail the LSAC at lsacinfo@lsac.org.

TEST PREPARATION

One good thing about the LSAT is that you do not need to spend months and months preparing for the exam. In fact, you should confine your preparation to no more than eight weeks of intensive work. Since the LSAT is not a knowledge-based examination, but rather tests how well you solve various sorts of problems, there is not a lot of material that you need to know to do well on the exam. The sorts of things that you do need to know are not fact based but are process based. They are often formulaic, and their application depends upon the test taker's recognition of the problem pattern presented.

My advice is to avoid professional preparation courses. These courses are expensive, often $900 or more, and their quality seems to vary dramatically with time and location, even within the same company. If you do take a professional preparation course, remember that you are still the one taking the exam. The company cannot take it for you, and you will not absorb the techniques and advice given if you do not take a highly active role in the program. Do not let the fact that you are taking a course act as a substitute for the work you need to do to score as well as possible on the LSAT.

However, everyone should get the sort of preparation necessary for them to do their best on the exam. If you feel the structured environment of a professional preparation course is the sort of thing you respond to best, then go ahead and spend the money without guilt. If you are well motivated, have sufficient free time, and organize your time well, your score will not significantly differ from the score you would manage with professional test preparation.

The LSAC found that the professionally prepped test taker on average scores only one point better than the person who self-prepared. If you conform to the average, that single point will not make any difference in how law schools treat you. Instead of spending $900 on a course, go to your local bookstore and purchase some LSAT preparation guides from reputable publishers. All of these guides have deficiencies, so you should purchase more than one. Spend a couple of weeks going over the guides at 2 to 3 hours per day, learning the different question types for the LSAT and the strategies employed in answering the questions. When you

My advice is to avoid professional preparation courses. These courses are expensive, often $900 or more, and their quality seems to vary dramatically with time and location, even within the same company.

feel you have a grasp on the different types of questions and at least a tentative feeling of how to answer them, then you should turn to taking practice exams.

Go ahead and take the practice exams in the guide books, but you want most of your test practice to take place with real LSATs. You can purchase these "back," or old, examinations directly from the LSAC through the contact information given earlier in this chapter. You should buy as many different examinations as are available. Buy them early, so that you do not have to be scrambling for practice exams a week before the test date. If the exams arrive before you are to begin your LSAT preparation, just leave them sealed, put them on a shelf, and forget about them. Do not take a peek or sneak looks at the answers. Just leave them alone. Then, beginning about three or so weeks before the exam date, schedule a practice exam every day. If possible, take the practice exams at the same time the real exam will take place. Keep track of the time religiously, and do not allow yourself to take even one second past the allotted time for each section. Better yet, let someone else be the timekeeper.

Make sure that you take one or two practice exams under less than ideal circumstances. Take an exam or two, say, in a cafeteria or in a common area with roommates. The LSAT environment is as quiet as possible, but that does not mean it is like a library. People do move around, and many times people are concentrating so hard they do not realize they are muttering under their breaths, groaning, or bouncing their feet up and down. Be prepared for these sorts of things, because if they distract you, they can obviously have a very bad effect on your performance. After you have taken a practice exam, score it immediately and analyze the questions you missed and try to correct any problems that might surface as a result of this analysis.

If you start three weeks or so before the actual exam, you will have around twenty practice tests to take. Take the last practice test two days before the exam date, and spend that evening and the next day relaxing or doing things you enjoy, but try not to think at all about the exam. Maybe have a beer or two at your favorite bar, or go catch a movie with some friends, or take a long hike. Whatever you do to relax, make sure it is something that will take your mind off of the examination.

It might be better to relax in the company of friends, since if you are alone you may descend into morbid contemplation of the LSAT. Make sure you get plenty of sleep the night before the examination. Lack of sleep is the quickest way to dull your senses and perform poorly on the exam. If this means going to bed a bit earlier to give yourself more time to fall asleep because of anxiety, then do it. When you get up in the morning, try not to change your normal routine. Do not, for example, experiment with breakfast food that is not in your normal diet. Do not gulp down eight cups of coffee to "wire" yourself up for the exam.

> **It might be better to relax in the company of friends, since if you are alone you may descend into morbid contemplation of the LSAT.**

TIPS FOR TAKING THE TEST

- Try to sign up for the June administration of the exam just prior to the fall semester in which you plan to apply to law school.

- Do not prepare for the exam months ahead of time. The LSAT is not a knowledge-based examination, but rather is meant to test the way in which you solve problems. Therefore, the test does not require months and months of preparation. In fact, over-preparation is a problem. If you over-prepare, you lose your "edge."

If you drink coffee, quit. Coffee will only accentuate the anxiety associated with the exam.

- Devote an intense period of four to six weeks in preparing for the exam. Order back examinations from the LSAC (these may be ordered using forms in the information and registration booklet). If you can afford it, and you are convinced that you need it, take a professional preparation course. Otherwise, buy self-help books from reputable publishers.

- Take your practice exams under test conditions. That is, time yourself and take a full examination each time. Remember, the test exams you get from LSAC will consist of only the four actually scored sections in each exam, but you will be taking five sections during the actual test. The LSAC adds the extra section to validate questions for future LSATs. The extra section does not count for your LSAT score, but you are not told which section is the validation section, so you must work on every section as if it counted. If you have attuned your body and mind to only sitting through four sections, it may create some trouble for you on the real exam when you ask your mind to stay focused longer than usual. To help with this problem, make sure you cannibalize some exams the week or so before you take the real exam and go through practice tests with five sections.

- Take one or two practice exams under less than ideal conditions. Take an exam in a cafeteria or other location that is likely to be noisy.

- If you drink coffee, quit. Coffee will only accentuate the anxiety associated with the exam. Further, it may cause you to make a trip to the bathroom during the exam—a catastrophic event—which will make you worry even more about how you are doing.

- Know yourself and your schedule. For example, to take up an indelicate matter, I once had a student who forgot that he had to use the restroom at virtually the same time of the morning every day. Needless to say, the student began to panic during the exam and felt so bad about the distraction he suffered that he canceled his exam score as soon as he returned home.

- Visit the room where the exam will be given before the day of the examination. Select several seats that appear to be satisfactory. Do not sit next to a window or in an aisle seat. Things going on outside the windows might distract you, and if you sit in an aisle seat, anybody who gets up in your row will have to climb past you. Try taking the corner seat farthest from the entrance to the room.

- Wear loose clothing, and spend a few seconds after sitting down to take several deep breaths and think of something restful. One student, who had on rather constricting clothing, reported that his leg fell asleep during the exam and that the discomfort suffered while the blood made its way back into his limb distracted him for several minutes.

- Prepare for the LSAT as you would prepare yourself for a sporting event—psych yourself up, and be "high" but controlled.

CANCELING YOUR SCORE AND RETAKING THE LSAT

Do not plan on retaking the LSAT. You should have it in your mind that this is a one-time experience and that you will never have to revisit the LSAT again. Obviously, if you take the exam more than once, it will cost you more time, money, and anguish. Nevertheless, there are times when canceling your score and retaking the exam are justified.

Canceling Your Score

You may cancel your LSAT score two ways. First, on the actual exam form, there is a place to indicate that you wish to have your test score canceled. You will not receive notification of cancellation until your test is processed along with all the other tests, around five to six weeks after the test is given. Further, if you fail to properly follow the cancellation instructions on the form, your test score will stand.

The second way to cancel your score is through written cancellation. You may use two methods to convey that written request. First, you may send a signed fax to the LSAC at 215-968-1119. Second, you may send an overnight letter or a score cancellation form, which is given out at the examination. Any other form of notification will not be accepted, since your signature is required to cancel your score.

When faxing or writing to cancel your score make sure that you take the following steps.

- Get your cancellation request to LSAC within *five business days after the exam*. This does not mean "in the mail." This means that the request must be in the LSAC's hands before the end of five business days after the exam.

- Include a clear statement that you wish to have your score canceled.

- State your name and social security number or Canadian Social Insurance number or a Law Services identification number.

- Provide the date you took the test and the center name and code number.

- Sign the communication.

- Have the letter or material to be faxed notarized.

- Obtain a sending confirmation sheet if you fax the request. If you send the request overnight, make sure you keep the paperwork so you can prove on what day the request was mailed if it is lost.

- Check back with the LSAC after a day or so to make sure they received the request.

- Make sure you receive a notice of cancellation from the LSAC.

If you cancel the exam during the administration using the space provided on the exam sheet, make sure you supplement this cancellation with a written cancellation within the five-business-day time period.

There are two general instances when you should cancel your score. First, you should probably cancel your score if you notice that there is something wrong with your exam sheet. For example, if you accidentally skipped a line early on in a section, and each of your subsequent answers are one line off, simply stop taking the exam. Hurrying around erasing multiple responses will increase your anxiety level, not to mention you may screw things up in your haste. Just stop taking the exam and send in the cancellation.

Second, you should probably cancel your score if you are genuinely sick during the exam. When I say genuinely sick, I mean sick enough so that your concentration is off and you are distracted. Do not cancel your score merely because you have a bad feeling about the exam or think that you "completely blew it." People who are very well prepared for the exam often have strong feelings that they have performed poorly. Frequently, students who feel this way will find their scores to be a personal best. Do not cancel your scores except for specific reasons.

Retaking the LSAT

The LSAC has found that people who retake the LSAT generally do better the second time around. On average, test retakers improve their performance by about two points. Does this mean that you should take the test twice or even more? No. Virtually all law schools use the mean score for applicants with multiple LSAT scores. If you do as the average person does and improve you score by two points, it will only prove a one point advantage when the schools figure the mean of the exams. One point higher on the LSAT represents no significant advantage in the application process.

If you already have a valid LSAT score, do not retake the exam unless the score you have is significantly under what you have been scoring on practice examinations. In making this determination, you must be honest with yourself. Ask yourself if you really were attentive in timing yourself accurately during practice exams. Did you sneak peeks at some questions and answers in your exams before taking them? If you can honestly say that your preparation was all on the up and up, then consider retaking the examination if there is more than a four-point disparity between your *average* practice exam score and the score you actually received.

If the disparity puts you at or below a 144 on the exam, then I suggest that you definitely sign up for another administration. The reason is that at 144 and below, you are on very dangerous footing and risk being completely boxed out of the admission process. Clearly, where you are on the scale of the exam also plays a part in determining whether or not to retake it. For example, if you have been scoring 175 on the exam and slip to a 171, I would not worry about it too much. Likewise, if you fall from a 139 to a 135, there will be little impact on your efforts to be admitted to law school.

If there is a huge disparity between two valid test scores, then it is only human nature to assume that "something happened" to cause the poor performance. Even though the scores will be averaged, the schools will be able to see each score individually. It makes sense to think that a person who scores a 150 on her first exam and a 168 on her second retook the exam precisely because of the disparity between practice exams and the score achieved on the first valid exam. In this case, there is such a difference that the tendency may be to ignore the bad score and see the better score as a more accurate indicator of the applicant's abilities. Notice, however, that things do not work well for the applicant if the scores are reversed—that is, if the high score comes first and the low score follows. If you have a score that is respectably reflective of your performance on practice examinations, just leave it alone and go on with your other admission activities.

If you already have a valid LSAT score, do not retake the exam unless the score you have is significantly under what you have been scoring on practice examinations.

Application Basics

Chapter 3

TIMING

LSDAS

The Law School Data Assembly Service (LSDAS) performs a number of crucial functions. The LSDAS evaluates your transcripts and prepares them in a uniform format, reports your Law School Admission Test (LSAT) scores, supplies copies of your transcripts and writing sample, and calculates your admission index for each school. If you so elect, you can pay an additional fee and have the LSDAS also send out copies of your letters of recommendation. It would be wise to make use of this option.

Registration for the LSDAS is required for all U.S. and most Canadian-trained applicants. Students trained in international institutions not listed in Appendix E of the application booklet are not permitted to make use of the services provided by the LSDAS. These students should consult directly with the law schools they are interested in applying to for further instructions.

Traditional Registration

Registration booklets for the LSAT and LSDAS for each upcoming test year are sent out in the spring. This gives you plenty of time to register for the LSAT and LSDAS services, and you should register early. If, as urged here, you are going to take the June administration of the LSAT, go ahead and sign up for the LSDAS at the same time.

When you register for the LSDAS, at about $100 or so, one free report to a school is included in the fee. Additional reports may be purchased at the time of registration at the rate of around $10 per school. If you wish to add schools later, it will cost you a bit more. If you follow the advice in this book, you should preregister for at least a dozen schools. The subscription to the LSDAS lasts for twelve months and may be renewed by submitting the appropriate form found in the application booklet.

Make sure you submit transcripts for all schools that you attended and which are listed in Appendix E of the registration booklet. Sometimes, students mistakenly think they need only submit transcripts from their degree-granting institution.

Also be aware that the LSDAS may not calculate your GPA the same way as your school does. For example, some schools allow grade replacement for certain courses or for courses at the freshman level. If both the original and the replacement grade appear on your transcript, then the LSDAS will count both grades in your GPA, even though your school may only use the replacement grade in its calculation. Also, grades such as WF (withdrawal failing) and U (unsatisfactory) are calculated as F grades by the LSDAS. About the only break you get is if you have failed the same class more than once; then the LSDAS only counts one F against you.

Have transcripts from all the schools you have attended that are listed in Appendix E of the application booklet sent to LSDAS, Box 2000-M, Newtown, Pennsylvania 18940-0993.

Online Registration

With a credit card, you may register for both the LSAT and LSDAS on line. In addition, the LSAC makes all of its informational guides and copies of back examinations available for purchase on line at the same site. If you have access to the Internet, go to http://www.lsac.org. If you do have access to the Web and a credit card, you should sign up with the LSAC on line. This will save you a lot of time, and you will not have to worry about whether or not your application got lost in the mail. Be prepared to print out all response pages to your application submissions and payment transactions so you will have a record of the event, just in case something goes terribly wrong with the LSAC server or Web site.

EXPENSE

Applying to law school is expensive. As mentioned earlier, the LSAT and the LSDAS will cost approximately $200. If you add a dozen or so prepaid LSDAS reports for the schools to which you intend to apply, you have already spent $300, and you have not even started the application process.

> **There are several things you can do to lower the cost of applying to law school, but too often, students are not very smart about *where* to cut costs.**

If you take a professional preparation course, that will cost you at least another $850. Add study aids and approximately $50 per school application fee, and you can easily spend $2,000 or more. There are several things you can do to lower the cost of applying to law school, but too often, students are not very smart about *where* to cut costs. For example, students seem to be almost universally offended by the perceived high application fees for applying to law school and frequently can be heard saying, "I can't afford to apply to more than three or four schools." This way of thinking is wrong and sends applicants off onto the path of disaster.

Application fees should not determine where and to how many schools you should apply. These determinations must be driven by your academic record, LSAT score, accomplishments, and personal characteristics and experiences.

There are three main ways to lower the cost of applying to law school. First, you may apply for a fee waiver from the LSAC. The fee waiver application may be ordered on line or may be available from your prelaw adviser. The LSAC uses the "absolute inability to pay" as its criterion for granting waivers and advises that only those applicants with "extreme need" apply. If you are successful in gaining a waiver, it will cover the cost of an LSAT exam, the annual subscription to the LSDAS, and the cost of one volume of LSAT preparedness material, known as TriplePrep Plus. In addition, if you are granted a waiver, law schools participating in the fee waiver program may waive their application fee. Successful fee waiver applications are very rare.

Second, you may apply for application fee waivers directly from the law schools to which you are applying. You may call or write to schools explaining who you are and what your financial situation is, backed up by evidence. Unless you can show that you will not be able to apply without the waiver, schools are likely to turn you down. Sometimes, schools are rude and testy with potential applicants who call up looking for a waiver.

Note that fee waiver member schools, as well as the LSAC, may process fee waiver requests, and so the criterion—being completely unable to pay—generally holds true across the board. There is an exception to this rule, though. Even if your fee waiver application is turned down by the LSAC, you can still talk to law schools individually if you have charac-teristics especially desired by the schools. For example, applicants who are members of ethnic minorities who are turned down for the fee-waiver program often receive appli-cation waivers when they contact schools individually. Fre-quently, applicants are solicited by schools to apply and are offered an application waiver as an inducement.

The third way you can reduce application costs is not to take a professional LSAT preparation course. These courses, no matter how well done, are of dubious value. They gener-ally meet once or twice a week and are not nearly as intense as is necessary to effect real improvement in the LSAT score. In the Law School Preparation Institute (LSPI) at the University of Texas at El Paso, the LSAT preparation phase lasts five weeks, 8 hours per day, six days a week. The students take upward of fifteen LSAT examinations under test-like conditions and are run through countless hours of logical problem solving. After the Institute, the students are tested weekly and have Saturday classes to keep them sharp until they have the LSAT out of the way. Even this prepara-tion, which is almost more than the average person is willing to tolerate, could be more intense. The LSPI has had great success, but it would be virtually impossible for a for-profit test preparation company to emulate the Institute. The cost of such a program would be prohibitive.

Also, the LSAC has determined that the difference in score between students who take professional preparation courses and those who do not averages about one point. This difference is insignificant and means that, on average, you are no better off for attending a professional preparation course compared to self-preparation.

If you feel you need the structure of a professional preparation course and can afford it, then go ahead and take

The LSAC has determined that the difference in score between students who take professional preparation courses and those who do not averages about one point. This difference is insignificant and means that you are no better off for attending a professional preparation course.

the course without guilt. Everyone should seek the help they need to do their best on the test. Chances are, though, you will do just as well if you self-prepare. See Chapter 2 for more discussion on this point.

LETTERS OF RECOMMENDATION

Be sure to line up potential recommenders early in the semester in which you are applying to law school. If you know or think there is a serious weakness in your application that can be dealt with by a recommender, lay out to the recommender the kind of problem it is and how you think it ought to be handled. Problems that might deserve special attention are low GPAs, series of poor grades, poor LSAT scores, and weak or disfavored majors. Remember that observations and comments from recommenders, even though everyone understands they are biased in your favor, are more effective than self-representations. The general rule is that if something would sound good coming from you, it will sound better coming from a recommender.

You should solicit at least three letters of recommendation. Some schools limit the number of letters they will accept to two. In one of the rare situations in which I council breaking a rule set up by a school, if you have three letters and they all have something important to say, then send them all along, even to the school that says to send no more than two letters.

Recommendation letters usually fall into one of several categories, and much of their effect on your admission to a school can be a matter of chance. At least two of your letters should be from academics or from people professionally trained to evaluate your writing skills and persuasive abilities.

An additional letter from a supervisor, lawyer, or judge who knows you and your work, or even a friend who can shed important light on your character, is nice to round out your application. But remember, the main importance of your letters of recommendation is to tout your academic skills. In what follows, we look at the various types of letters and what they may do for you.

Letters from Your Professors

Letters from instructors are the most common letters found in application packages. You should begin thinking of which professors you want to ask for letters early—during the spring semester of your junior year. Please be aware that it is not necessary for the professor to know you well or even remember you, though it is better. If you supply a brief resume, describe the courses you have taken from the professor, and enclose tests or papers from the course, most professors will agree to write a letter. On this score, never throw away your old papers or exams.

Obviously, try to select professors from whom you have received A grades. At the very beginning of the fall semester in which you will be applying for law school, meet with your prelaw adviser and tell her the names of professors you plan to ask for letters of recommendation. You should do this because your adviser may know things that you do not, such as if the professor you planned to ask for a letter did not win tenure and is no longer at the university, took another job, or is in Spain for the year.

Sometimes, students ask whether or not there is any difference between a letter from a full professor and a letter from an assistant professor or even a part-time lecturer. Unless you have a very famous professor in whose class you

General letters, with sentences such as, "John is one of the best students I have had in recent history," are not very useful. Specifics should be conveyed.

did well, go ahead and ask for letters from those instructors you feel will write you the best letters.

A bigger problem for students is professors who agree to write letters but simply do not understand what sorts of things law schools want to see. General letters, with sentences such as, "John is one of the best students I have had in recent history," are not very useful. Specifics should be conveyed. For example, if John received an A grade in the class or classes he took with the recommender, where does that put him in the universe of students similarly situated? How many people make A grades in that class or classes? If the instructor can say "John made an A in my macroeconomics course and, historically, only 4 percent of my students make such a grade in that class," then the law schools have been told something important about John relative to other students.

Appendix D includes a list of guidelines to professors that is put out by the Law School Preparation Institute at UTEP. It is not a bad idea to gently let your recommenders know the sorts of things that law schools wish to hear about. Also, be sure to go through the checklist at the end of this chapter.

Letters from Famous People

Occasionally, applicants want to know if they should have a famous friend or acquaintance write them a letter of recommendation. These letters may be desirable, but the first rule for applicants concerning letters of recommendation is that the recommender should know the subject of the recommendation well and must be able to convey specifics of his character and abilities. A letter from a U.S. senator does you no good if it starts out, "I never met Mr. ____, but I understand he worked in one of my home offices one summer."

Furthermore, law professors are often very independent, taciturn, and iconoclastic people. They do not like to think they are being muscled or scammed, and they will be unimpressed with a big name that does not have anything useful to say about an applicant. If a famous person does know you well, you must decide what information that person can convey about you that is useful for law school admission purposes. You may be friends with a movie star, but this does not mean that actor can say anything of value about you to a law school. Matters of interest to law schools concern communication skills, ability to analyze complex problems, integrity, reliability, civility, and commitment.

Your friend may be able to say very nice things about your integrity, civility, and reliability, and this would make a perfectly fine letter of recommendation. Bear in mind, though, that the main meat of your letters must emphasize your academic skills, particularly your writing skills and abilities to reduce complicated arguments to useable chunks that you can then apply in a persuasive manner for or against some proposition. The letter from the famous friend is perfectly fine if it addresses your personal qualities, but one such letter is plenty. The other letters should focus on your academic skills.

Letters from Lawyers and Judges

It does not hurt to have a letter from a lawyer or judge who can comment on your personal characteristics and abilities. But again, avoid the letter from a person who has not had close enough contact with you to evaluate you in a manner useful for law school admission purposes.

Be warned that some of the worst letters of recommendation ever seen come from lawyers and judges. You must remind your recommender that the focus of the letter needs to be on you, not on a stroll down memory lane or a bitter diatribe against law schools.

Often, letters in this category present another problem; the letter will be coming from a family member. Do not have family members write letters of recommendation for you, unless the letter is written specifically to the member's alma mater and it is a school to which you are applying. Sometimes, though, family members insist on helping. In this case, have the family member send the letter of recommendation to your career office at campus, and then just ignore the file.

Be warned that some of the worst letters of recommendation ever seen come from lawyers and judges.

Letters from Supervisors and Friends

Letters from supervisors or others you have worked with or for are perfectly fine, as long as the recommender focuses on your work habits and personal characteristics. Such letters should center around an applicant's maturity, demonstrated responsibility, reliability in showing up for work, initiative in solving problems and handling tasks without supervision, communication skills, relationships with other office personnel, integrity, and so forth.

Letters from friends may use the same approach as letters from supervisors and workers, though there should be no effort to hide the nature of the relationship. The recommender should just come out and say, "Mr. X is my best friend." As you might imagine, letters from friends will not count as much as letters from supervisors and academics. Certainly, your packet can do without such a letter, but if it seems like the right thing to do, make sure that there is no more than one letter like this in your application material.

Letter of Recommendation Checklist

- See your prelaw adviser and notify her about whom you wish to ask for letters of recommendation.

- Solicit letters around the September 1 of the fall in which you will apply to law school. Ask the potential recommender straight out if she can write you an excellent letter. If she waffles or says "no" to this query, thank the person and move on to another potential recommender. Set a deadline for the letter by suggesting that you will come pick it up on October 1. If you do not suggest a date, many professors will simply put it out of their minds.

- Supply recommenders with a brief resume, a list of classes you have had with the recommender (if any), grades you made in the classes, and any tests or papers that went to satisfy course requirements.

- Recommenders should know that letters should be no more than two pages—less if possible. These letters should make their points quickly and clearly.

- Let the recommender know what it is law schools wish to hear about.

- If you have a low GPA or LSAT score, ask the recommender to comment on your abilities relative to these objective marks. For example, if you scored in the thirtieth percentile on the LSAT, ask the recommender to comment on whether or not this is indicative of your abilities as demonstrated in her classes.

- Make things easy for the recommender. For example, do not ask for a separate letter for each school; a general letter will suffice. Also, make sure that you give the recommender all of the material at one time. Do not string out recommendation requests for schools two or three at a time. Also, make sure that, where necessary, you have affixed proper postage to envelopes and filled in the address. The LSDAS provides a service that will send out letters of recommendation to each school an applicant applies to along with the applicant's LSDAS and LSAT data. You should use this service. This way the recommender need send only one letter out—the one that goes to the LSDAS master file.

- Even though you may have your letters of recommendation sent to the distribution service offered by LSDAS, note that many schools require that a recommender form also be filled out by each person writing you a letter. Sometimes these forms ask for ratings of the applicant in various areas. You will still have to obtain these forms and have the recommenders fill them out and send them in to the schools or return them to you to be placed in with your application even if you do take advantage of the LSDAS letter service.

THE PERSONAL STATEMENT

Nothing gives students more problems in the law school application process than the personal statement. Virtually all schools require or allow applicants to submit a personal statement. Some of the most tortured English appears in the personal statements of applicants to law school. Students are often unaware of the role the personal statement plays in the application process and end up over-worrying about this item. In most applications, the personal statement is of little importance. Some will not be read, many will be skimmed, and very few will be scrutinized.

The reason you must take pains with the statement is that, even though it is not likely to help you be admitted to law school, it can surely hurt your chances for admission. A skimmed statement that is poorly written and shows little polish and organization will impart a bad opinion about your entire application. In addition, though the statement is almost always of little importance in deciding whether or not to admit a student, there are times when it is a crucial document in your application packet.

First, if you are a member of an ethnic minority group, the chances are extremely high that your personal statement is going to be looked at rather carefully by someone in the admission process. Therefore, all ethnic minority applicants should make sure to have a first-rate personal statement.

Second, it is possible that if a school places your application in a category that warrants neither presumptive admission or rejection, there may be members of the admission committee who will at least scan your letter with some care. Furthermore, if you are in contention for one of the last slots in a class, your application packet, including your personal statement, is likely to be subjected to greater scrutiny.

Third, if you have unusual experiences and you write about them well, your personal statement may attract the attention of an admission committee member who may then become your champion.

Some of the most tortured English appears in the personal statements of applicants to law school.

Remember that the reader is looking first to evaluate your writing skills and second to get a feel for what sort of person you are. Represent yourself as you see yourself, not as what you think the reader would like to see.

There are a number of pitfalls to avoid when writing your statement. Particularly, there are two kinds of personal statements to avoid. The first type to avoid is the Why-I'm-So-Great personal statement. Many students, who are unaccustomed to writing about and describing themselves to strangers, assume that they must go to ridiculous lengths to sell themselves to the reader. The brightest, most humble student will end up writing a personal statement that would make people with Napoleon complexes blush in embarrassment. Remember that the reader is looking first to evaluate your writing skills and second to get a feel for what sort of person you are. Represent yourself as you see yourself, not as what you think the reader would like to see.

Another sort of statement to avoid is the laundry-list letter. Too often, this type of statement results from the conclusion by the applicant that he really does not have anything to say about himself. Your personal statement should not be a grab bag of all the things you have done in your life. These accounts are also singularly uninteresting. Information about charitable work, club membership, offices held, etc., should appear in the application proper. Remember that it is important to grab the reader's attention.

Think of the personal statement as a mini-paper or a very short story about some feature of your life. It should have a thesis, though an implied thesis works better in this situation; a development phase; and a conclusion. It should be no more than 450 words and, if possible, should fit on a single sheet of paper. Do not, however, make the font so small as to be unreadable in trying to reduce it to one page in length. Try to make the opening sentence catchy, but don't make it sound ridiculous or pompous. A short account of some important event in your life is perfectly fine for the personal statement. The idea is to tell the law school a lot about yourself without talking about yourself.

It is extremely difficult to describe a good personal statement, so I have included two actual personal statements submitted with applications by students who have recently applied to law school. Both of these statements are effective and well written, but what sets them apart from other equally well-written statements is their simplicity, directness, and honesty. The first of these statements is quite long, much longer than might be normally tolerated. If you have little to say, then say it in few words. But if you have something to say, a story to tell about yourself, then go ahead and exceed the suggested or even required limits set out by the school. Try to stay as close as possible to the limit, but do not denude your statement of its interesting points merely to comply with a word limit.

Life experiences that are interesting enough to allow you to ignore a word limit are difficult to identify at first. Many times, people think their lives are extraordinarily interesting and worthy of detailed recounting, when in fact they are not. You should give your statement to your prelaw adviser for suggestions before you send it out to your schools.

DEAN CERTIFICATION

Dean certification forms are a bit anachronistic, but some schools still require them before they will process your application. Sometimes, students are confused and think that the law schools are asking a dean to write you a letter of recommendation. The dean certification form is not a letter of recommendation, and it is not required that the dean even know who you are. Usually, the dean that handles these forms is the Dean of Students or another official responsible for student affairs.

The primary purpose of the form is to establish at least a baseline of good conduct at your school. For example, the form is meant to elicit information about any probationary status a student might have once been on, school suspensions or even expulsions, punishment for scholastic violations, instances of disruptive behavior, and so forth. Just drop the form off at the dean's office and the dean's staff will fill it out, including any derogatory information, and mail it out. Check with the dean's office to make sure there was no derogatory information included on your form. Dean's offices do make mistakes and get students confused. If you find out that there was such information included and you did not expect this to be the case, ask the dean what the information was and how it got into your file. If the dean did include derogatory information about you, then you will need to prepare an explanation for the information and submit it to the school with your application.

STUDENT DIVERSITY

Insuring student diversity is a primary aim of the admission committees at all law schools. "Student diversity" is not a euphemism for minority recruitment, though there is often a strong focus in that area. Law schools truly want to assemble classes that have as much geographical, academic, experiential, gender, and ethnic diversity as is practicable. In trying to assemble this diverse set of students, admission committee members take into account a myriad of items other than GPA and LSAT score. Although it remains true that GPA and the LSAT score are the most important items in the package, an applicant's entire packet may offer such substantial diversity that it overcomes a weak index score and garners admission.

Class diversity can be divided into two broad categories: diversity that is driven by moral imperatives and diversity that is driven by instructional concerns. The admission of students from ethnicities that have traditionally suffered and continue to suffer racist treatment, especially where such treatment was a matter of governmental policies and de jure rules, is considered a moral imperative for admission committees. The three most obvious groups of ethnic minorities to match these features are African Americans, Mexican Americans, and Native Americans. Hispanics from origins other than Mexico, such as Puerto Rico, may receive admission preference, but usually not to the degree of that received by Mexican Americans.

Obviously, there are members of many groups that do not receive favored admission yet have been subject to racist treatment. Approximately 130,000 Japanese Americans were interned in "concentration camps" during WWII for no reason other than their ethnic background. Most of these people were U.S. citizens who were never indicted of a crime but were imprisoned and had their property taken. Despite this, Japanese Americans usually do not receive admission preferences.

Precious little thinking and writing has focused on what constitutes a group that should receive preference. The scale of racism, longevity of the racist practice, current economic

The admission of students from ethnicities that have traditionally suffered and continue to suffer racist treatment, especially where such treatment was a matter of governmental policies and de jure rules, is considered a moral imperative for admission committees.

situation of the ethnic group in question, and representation in the legal community, among other considerations, seem to mainly determine which groups receive favored admission treatment.

Admission Preference

The most common law student tends to be about 23 years old, white, and male. Many law students have never had full-time jobs, and the first such job they will have will be as a lawyer. Consequently, law schools usually give slightly favorable admission breaks to students who are ethnic minorities in groups with favored admission status, nontraditional students, and applicants who have interesting experiences or backgrounds. If you are in one of these categories, your chances for admission at schools outside the range of your numbers increase, but decisions become more idiosyncratic.

In essence, if you have reasonable numbers, you are no longer competing against the entire applicant pool for a school. You may be competing against other applicants who are members of ethnic minority groups or nontraditional students. So, if you are an ethnic minority applicant, a nontraditional student, or someone with unusual life experiences, you may want to shoot higher than you normally would. See Chapter 5 concerning the number of schools to apply to.

Ethnic minority applicants often react to admission breaks with a feeling of guilt that they will be using their ethnicity to gain admission to law school. Perhaps your first lesson as an attorney is that you use whatever weapons you have available to win your case. Law schools give preference to veterans, women, nontraditional students, single mothers, and a host of other applicants; they do this because it is the best thing for the school. In three years, a law school has to take a group of mostly young people, who often have never had a full-time job, and prepare them to take responsibility for the property, affairs, and, sometimes, lives of their clients. One aid in this process is the development of a diverse class with students of varying backgrounds and experience.

Preferences in admission are designed to help all law students mature and learn together. Admission preferences are not a handout; you must expect to go to law school with the intention of sharing your background, experiences, and cultural and ethnic traditions with the rest of your classmates.

INTERVIEWS

Very few schools give interviews, and it is easy to see why. Interviews take up an extraordinary amount of time, personnel, and money. In addition, since in law school most of the admission decisions are made by faculty members, faculty members would probably be the primary conductors of interviews. Few faculty members are willing or able to make such a commitment of time.

Another reason to disfavor interviews is that, unless a school is prepared to bring students to the school or send admission people to the students, then the only people to interview at a school will be those that can afford to make the trip. This would unfairly exclude poorer people from taking part in a crucial admission opportunity. Nevertheless, some schools recognize that the interview is perhaps the best evaluative device an admission committee has. Due to growing uneasiness and changing conditions in the law governing admission, a trickle of schools has started to utilize interviews.

This trickle may be followed by a flood, and, in the future, we could see many schools willing to augment application materials with interviews of candidates.

For example, most of the law schools in Texas have discussed adopting some sort of protocol for interviewing candidates, and the University of Texas at Austin has aggressively pursued interviews with applicants for the past two years. It is true that many interview programs are directed at recruiting member of minority groups, but not exclusively so.

You must be careful of interviews since they can work against you as well as for you. It would be wrong to see interviews as an opportunity if you are someone who does not do well in interviews. Part of the problem is that applicants often have no idea whether or not they interview well because they have never been through an interview. Most universities and colleges have career centers that will put you through mock interviews. Usually, these centers will also give you advice on dress, comportment, and other matters of importance when interviewing. If you do go on an interview pay attention to the following points.

You must be careful of interviews since they can work against you as well as for you. It would be wrong to see interviews as an opportunity if you are someone who does not do well in interviews. Part of the problem is that applicants often have no idea whether or not they interview well because they have never been through an interview.

- Dress appropriately.

- Greet the interviewer with a handshake.

- Address the interviewer by title and name (Ms. ___, Dr. ___, etc.). Since interviewers usually say their name at the beginning of the interview when you will be at your most nervous, make sure that you catch the name. If you forget, just ask.

- Sit appropriately, with squared shoulders, facing the interviewer. Do not slump or lounge about.

- Pay careful attention to what you do with your hands. It is best to keep them folded on a table or in your lap. Most important, do not drum your fingers, twirl your hair, or otherwise fidget.

- Watch what you say. Avoid saying "um," "ya'know what I mean?," "catch my drift?," "basically," and other phrases and habits of language that may seem unattractive.

- Make eye contact with the interviewer, or, if there is more than one interviewer, make sure you make eye contact with all of them rather than focusing all of your attention on one person.

- Answer the questions asked. Frequently, applicants wander off into fields unknown, never addressing the subject posed by the interviewer's question or questions.

- Make sure your speaking voice is the appropriate volume to be easily heard by all present.

- It is OK to chuckle or even guffaw, but do not succumb to a belly laugh, no matter what the interviewer says. Some of the most shocking and annoying sounds are emitted by laughing humans.

- Be complete but concise in your responses. Do not drone on and on. You should never take more than four or five sentences to answer a question, unless you receive cues from the interviewer to keep talking.

- Do not respond to questions by nodding or shaking your head; make complete verbal responses to questions.

- Do not bring up personal matters or anything that might make the interviewer feel uncomfortable, unless you are specifically asked about the subject. Sometimes, interviewers will ask you about things in your personal statement that might otherwise make for uncomfortable conversation between strangers. As long as the interviewer wishes to talk about something, you should comply, but wait for the interviewer to bring these subjects up.

- Make sure that you also act as an interviewer. Have a number of questions prepared and in your head ready to ask. If the interview becomes uncomfortable or long silences occur, shift the conversation around to questions about the school, the faculty, or the library.

- Always thank the interviewer and shake hands upon leaving. Do not ask the interviewer how you did or whether or not you have a good chance of admission. If the interviewer wishes to bring these things up, great, but you should not pursue the matter.

ELECTRONIC APPLICATIONS

I recommend that you stay away from electronic submission of applications for the following reasons. First, it will cause duplication of work if you decide to purchase, as indeed you should, the application CD-ROM from the LSAC. Second, it is a lot easier to make mistakes in an electronic format and then to miss them while going back over the application. Of course, one can print out the application and go over it carefully, but then one has to consider whether or not any advantage has been realized from the electronic process if you go to all this trouble. Third, I do not trust the schools not to lose or, more likely, screw up an electronically submitted application.

The legal world has never been known to be on the cutting edge of technology use and is indeed quite conservative when it comes to incorporating new electronic devices into its processes. More specifically, there are some very sloppy and unstable and insecure Web sites put up by law schools. For example, not long ago the Web site of one of the most competitive law schools was a total disaster. Links would not work, HTML was not checked for how it would appear on various platforms, and forms downloaded either incorrectly or not at all.

In the very near future, these problems are sure to be resolved, and soon we will not have to worry about the sort of problems brought up here. However, for the time being, go with the application CD-ROM from the LSAC. Even if all of the law school sites were completely trustworthy, it would still be best to use the LSAC's CD-ROM in applying to law school. With all of the applications to schools in a single place and core data about an applicant entered automatically on all applications, it is difficult to match for ease and saving time. Note, though, that the CD-ROM may not have all of the forms you need for each school. For example, it may still be necessary to obtain recommender and dean certification forms directly from some schools. In this case, you may be able to download these forms from the school's Web site and print them.

> **The legal world has never been known to be on the cutting edge of technology use and is indeed quite conservative when it comes to incorporating new electronic devices into its processes.**

WHEN DO YOU HEAR BACK?

If you have submitted your applications by December 1, you can start hearing back from schools as early as the middle of January. More likely, though, responses will begin to trickle in at the end of February and can continue all the way through May or after. This part of the process is agony, as there is nothing left for you to do to take your mind off concerns about admission. You have completed all the tests and applications and you are left to try to focus on your last-semester courses while various committees at various institutions are using arcane and secretive means to decide your fate.

Many applicants make the waiting even worse by repeatedly calling schools and asking where their application is in the admission process. You should receive a card from each school that tells you when your application is complete, and you should call those schools that have not sent you such a notification by February 1 (provided you had your applications in by December 1). You should not call the school after you have received this notification. Schools will not lose your records or your application. They go through this process year in and year out and are generally very professional in how they conduct it. Save yourself heightened anxiety and make things easier on the schools by leaving them alone.

Occasionally, applicants believe that a phone call from their member of Congress or a judge that they know can move things along in their favor. This is almost always a very bad idea and should not even be contemplated. Law schools are not impressed by this kind of contact. Sometimes, though, it is the parents of the applicant who are worried the most. Fathers and mothers will tell their children things such as "Your Aunt Maggie is a Nebraska alum. I'm going to get her to shake up the admission office and find out what is going on and taking so long." You must make clear to your family and friends that you may not hear from schools for many months and that waiting for such a period of time does not indicate that anything is wrong with the people who staff the admission committees. Also note that, for most applicants, quick responses usually mean rejection. Try to relax and let things happen without trying to control them.

POSITION DEPOSITS AND WAITING LISTS

Position Deposits

Handling position deposits is relatively straightforward. Suppose school Y admits you to its program and says that you must have a $250 deposit submitted and postmarked by April 15 in order to reserve a position in that fall's class. If April 15 nears and you have no other offers, then send in the deposit. If you have had a better offer, send the deposit to that school and let your position lapse at school Y. The next chapter deals with how to figure out which school is better.

Do not make the mistake of assuming that a better offer is sure to come in and let the deadline for school Y pass with no other offers available. After you have sent in the deposit to the best school you are admitted to prior to the deadline, you can simply wait and leap frog when and if other offers come in. You may have sent the deposit in to school Y but now you have a better offer from school X. Send in the deposit to X. Submitting a deposit is not a promise that you will attend the school; it is merely a fee for holding open the chance to make such a promise further down the road.

Occasionally, students feel bad that they have sent a deposit in to school Y but have decided to go to school X. They feel as if they have gone back on their word or at least reneged on an implied promise. Sure, some schools are not

Do not make the mistake of assuming that a better offer is sure to come in and let the deadline for school Y pass with no other offers available.

going to relieve you of that feeling in the hopes it will cause you to show up in their beginning fall class, but the applicant is under no obligation to attend a school for merely submitting a deposit. The schools know the game, and you should, too. The deposit is designed to test an applicant's seriousness as a prospect so schools can calculate potential class numbers and to create a feeling of commitment in the applicant. You should also know that deposits submitted to schools that you do not attend are nonrefundable.

Waiting Lists

On rare occasions, an applicant will not know whether or not she has been admitted to a school until the first day of class. In this case, the applicant has been "wait listed." Usually, applicants are given more warning than a single day, but a wait list can go right up to the last minute. If you are wait listed, you should try to find out as much information as possible about how the list is cleared. For example, some schools have multiple lists. You may be on wait list one for out-of-state students. Find out how much of wait list one has ultimately been offered admission in the past. Usually, secretaries know this information, and, if you are polite, they may help you. On the other hand, placement on some waiting lists is tantamount to rejection, and you should be aware that these lists are constructed to meet the school's need in filling up the incoming class, not the convenience of the applicant. That is why you may be on a list that has not been tapped in the previous history of the school, but because there is a *theoretical* possibility that the list may be used, it must be filled out. This leads to false hope and a lot of anxiety spent uselessly. This is why you must do your best to find out how the waiting lists work at those schools that have "waited" you.

REJECTIONS

Unless you score above 170 on the LSAT and have close to a perfect GPA, you are going to be rejected by some of the schools to which you apply. Even if you have these big numbers, you may be treated to a rejection or two anyway. Rejection will cause an applicant to be disappointed and, frequently, angry. After the initial shock wears off, and if the rejection is early on in the process, applicants begin to wonder if they had somehow screwed up applications to all of the schools and will be rejected by the lot. This may set up a period of debilitating anxiety and moodiness that can only be cured when an offer of admission from a desired school arrives.

You must prepare yourself for rejection ahead of time. Tell yourself that when you get dumped by Berkeley you are going to celebrate with a nice dinner and a ritualistic burning ceremony where you torch the rejection letter. Do not dwell on the rejections. Do not call those schools that have rejected you and demand to know why you were not accepted. Just forget about the bad news.

It is hard not to read things into a rejection, but do not take it personally. Admission decisions are merely guesses, predictions of what seems to be best for the entering class. Mistakes are frequently made. Remember, application to law

> **You must prepare yourself for rejection ahead of time. Tell yourself that when you get dumped by Berkeley you are going to celebrate with a nice dinner and a ritualistic burning ceremony where you torch the rejection letter. Do not dwell on the rejections.**

school is a game of numbers, a play on probability. That is why students should never have their heart set on a particular school, though it is perfectly OK, based on one's numbers, to have one's heart set on getting into one of a *group* of schools.

REAPPLICATION

Infrequently, students must go through a second application season. This usually occurs for one of two reasons. The first, and most obvious, is when the student receives no offer of admission. If you follow the advice in this book, the chances of this happening are greatly decreased. Nevertheless, it still happens.

The first inclination of students who have received no admission offers is to be bitter about the schools that rejected them and to avoid reapplying to those schools the second time around. This is a mistake. There is a fair amount of evidence that the chances of admission go up for the applicant upon reapplicaiton. At any rate, for the second time around, you should not significantly change the list of schools you are applying to, so long as the list originally was consistent with your numbers and amenable to the opinion of your prelaw adviser. If you do anything, you should increase the number of schools to which you apply. If you find yourself in this situation, before reapplying make sure you go through the checklist included at the end of this section.

The second situation where you should consider reapplication is if you received offers from only the least desirable schools you applied to but your numbers indicate that you should have done better. In other words, in your four-category application spread (see Chapter 5) you received no offers of admission from schools in your top three categories. In this case, you have the choice of attending a school that is lower on your list or taking another crack at your favorite schools.

If you reapply, it will cost you an extra year, but this should not worry you too much. To be on the safe side, you should accept admission at the school highest on your list that admitted you and then ask for a year deferment. Most law schools will give a student a one-year deferment without causing too much trouble or asking too many questions. Usually, the claim that there are personal matters you need to sort out is sufficient. Then go through the reapplication process during the next cycle and, if you get into a school you find more desirable, then cancel your deferment and accept admission at the school you like better. If history repeats itself, then you are no worse off than you were before; only a year off schedule. At any rate, before making any decision not to go to school and to go through another application cycle, you must talk to your prelaw adviser and go through the items on the following checklist.

- Have your personal statement reevaluated by your prelaw adviser. Listen to what your adviser recommends and make the suggested changes, if there are any. Students sometimes hurt themselves by submitting, over adviser's objections, strange and terrible personal statements. Do not be obstinate.

- Determine if anything in your letters of recommendation is unfavorable. On rare occasions, a recommender will write a letter that is derogatory or scathing; all the while, the applicant is laboring under the illusion that the recommender has written a favorable letter. A very bad letter is hard for an admission committee

On rare occasions, a recommender will write a letter that is derogatory or scathing; all the while, the applicant is laboring under the illusion that the recommender has written a favorable letter. A very bad letter is hard for an admission committee to get past and can exert a lot of influence on admission decisions.

to get past and can exert a lot of influence on admission decisions. This recommendation brings up some touchy issues; since applicants generally waive their right to see letters of recommendation, it is not ethical for them to go back on this promise. You may have your letters sent by each recommender to your prelaw adviser. The adviser, without revealing the contents of the letters, can suggest that you drop a particular letter. Even this borders on an ethical violation. On the other hand, you should not be forced to endure a second round of applications with a letter that is unfavorable. After all, you get to select the recommenders, and it represents your chance to have faculty members and others for whom you feel you have done good work to argue in your behalf. You should consult your adviser about this matter before taking any action.

- Have friends or family members go over your applications looking for glaring errors or unfavorable features that you might have missed.

- Go over your transcripts to insure that all of your grades are correctly reported by your undergraduate schools and that the grades are correctly recorded by the LSDAS. Also, make sure that your GPA at each undergraduate school is correctly calculated. LSDAS seems not to make mistakes, but it could happen.

- Make sure that the LSAT score reported to the schools by the LSDAS is the same score you received on your score report notice. Again, the LSAC seems not to make mistakes, but it does not hurt to check.

- Check the residency status you have been placed in by the various schools. For example, in many states, residents of the state applying to public law schools are given an admission preference. If you are incorrectly classified as a nonresident, you will not get the preference. In some cases, this preference is enormous. For example, in Texas, the University of Texas at Austin may only admit 20 percent nonresidents into each class. This means that the numbers for an out-of-state applicant must be higher than those required of in-state residents.

How Law Schools Evaluate Your Application

Chapter 4

APPLICATION APPEARANCE

Clean and Neat

First, you need to make sure that the application is clean and free of smudges, marks, dirt, and other matter that would lead an admission committee member to believe that you are sloppy or careless. Most faculty and staff members are very proud of their schools and their colleagues, and any application that seems not to treat them with the respect they feel they deserve will be in for a hard time. A sloppy application tells an admission committee member that you are so careless and unattuned to detail and apparently have so little regard for her school that you cannot even submit a clean application.

Never submit a handwritten application, even if the school says such submissions are allowable. The application should be oriented toward ease of use, and even the best handwriting is more difficult to read than typed or printed applications. Again, a handwritten application conveys a certain sense of sloppiness and carelessness.

If you are going to use application forms sent to you from the schools, then you should do the following. As soon as each application arrives, carefully make three photocopies of each page on a clean photocopy machine. Then, put the real application away in a safe place where the dogs, cats, mice, children, and rain water cannot reach it. Take the first photocopy of the application and fill it out by hand, making sure that you answer all questions completely and concisely. Then, take your second copy and type up the application, making sure that all answers to questions fit in the margins and are grammatically correct. Finally, the third copy should be carefully typed and used as a template from which to fill out the actual application. Again, put the actual application in a safe place until it is ready to be delivered.

An easier method for applying to law school, though, is to purchase the "Applications on CD-ROM" from the LSAC. This CD is reasonably priced and is usually available in mid-September to late September in order to give time for law schools to submit their final application versions. The LSAC describes this service in the following way:

> "The LSACD is a Windows-compatible, interactive multimedia CD-ROM that makes it easy and efficient to explore law schools, discover the best ones for you, and use your computer to fill out your applications.
>
> One hundred eighty-one ABA-approved U.S. law schools are included in the LSACD's fully searchable database and easy-to-use application forms. Our core information section and flow-as-you-go technology save you the time and trouble of having to fill out the same information over and over—you answer the core questions once, select the schools to which you want to apply, and let the program place the answers in the proper fields. The

LSACD also makes it easy for you to write
and edit your essays and personal statements
so that you can target them for each school."

Using this product will cure most of your application appearance problems and will save you a lot of time and trouble. Nevertheless, there are also several other issues to consider in regard to application appearance.

Filled Out Correctly and Completely

Obviously, you must make sure that each application is filled out correctly and completely, but this can be trickier than may first appear. Read each question carefully and all the way through. Often, with forms, we tend to jump to conclusions without fully reading the instructions. Some law school application questions have multiple parts, and each part needs to be addressed. Make sure you understand how personal statements and other matter on separate pages are to be sent with the application. If you do not understand a question, refer to the accompanying instructions, if any. If you still cannot find out what is wanted, contact the school's admission office. Finally, do not leave a question unanswered because you did not feel like talking about the subject or believed that the question was optional. If answering a question is optional, the application will make that clear.

Syntax, Vocabulary, and Grammar

Be sure to use standard English in responding to questions on applications. Do not abbreviate responses or clip them. For example, do not write things such as, "Work/Full time/ Bus driver—Wildcat Sch. Dist." Make sure your answers are in complete, grammatically correct sentences free of all but universally recognizable abbreviations.

If columns are given by the school, such as *Employer,* *Dates of Employment,* and *Job Duties,* then go ahead and put the normal clipped responses for each job under the columns; however, do not create your own schema for abbreviation. Also, be careful of syntax, especially when filling out applications on line or with the CD-ROM service from the LSAC. Syntax and vocabulary in e-mails, chat rooms, and even online forms are often quite different from what we encounter on matter that is physically published on paper—books and the like. Make sure you do not adopt a tone or approach that is inappropriately casual for the job at hand. Finally, have someone read over the application and your responses. Frequently, a fresh set of eyes will see things you have missed.

Photographs

Some schools request or require that each applicant submit a photograph with the application. Most schools, though, do not have such a requirement and never mention a thing about including photographs. You should clip a small photograph to the corner of your application. Humans are peculiarly ocular animals; much of our lives revolves around visual perception. Many people feel more comfortable going over an application that includes a photograph of the applicant, and it probably will not hurt you to provide a small photograph with each of your applications. Do not include the 8x10 glossy of you with 162 friends and relatives at your family reunion replete with a red circle to identify you. Make sure the photograph is only of you and is a head shot, such as you see on passports and identification cards.

Occasionally, applicants desire to or actually do submit a videotape of themselves talking about themselves. The theory is that "if the schools just get to know me, they will

You should clip a small photograph to the corner of your application. Many people feel more comfortable going over an application that includes a photograph.

love me and express that love by taking me into their program." It is doubtful that such tapes do applicants much good. It is very unlikely that committee members will look at these tapes, and even if one or more do, it may not have the result the applicant desires. We are so attuned to looking at professionally produced and manufactured tapes that an amateur job can come off looking quite bad. Forget the videotape and go with the passport photo.

INCONSISTENCIES AND PREVARICATION

Before you create the final application for each school, go over everything you have said with an eye to consistency. Make sure that what you say in one part of the application does not contradict something you have said elsewhere. For example, if you say you have worked too much to undertake charitable activities during school, but elsewhere say you go rock climbing at least twice a week, you have a bit of explaining to do. It is OK not to give your free time to charitable endeavors, but it is not OK to say that you cannot give such time because you are too busy working and then, in another part of the application, go into detail about your frequent rock-climbing exploits. Such answers border on prevarication and lying, and, for obvious reasons, you do not want the readers to think of you as a liar.

More often, though, inconsistencies are the result of incomplete answers and explanations or the failure to specify time frames accurately. So, again, go over your application looking for inconsistencies between answers. Have a friend or family member also read over the application with an eye to discovering these sorts of discrepancies.

INDEX SCORE

As mentioned above, each school uses its own formula to calculate an index score for each applicant. Please refer to Chapter 1 for a more in-depth discussion of how index scores are used. Your index score at each school is function of your LSAT score and your GPA. Many schools have built-in allowances for science majors versus liberal arts majors and formulas to kick up scores for students from exceptional undergraduate schools.

The index score is a way of rank ordering the entire applicant pool. This is just the beginning of the evaluation of each applicant, but it is an important beginning. After rank ordering the applicants, usually each school will arrive at two threshold scores. The first threshold score represents the lower-limit index score at which the school is willing to seriously entertain an applicant for acceptance. Applicants with index scores below this threshold, which may change from year to year, depending upon the pool of applicants, are placed in the "presumptive denial" category. The second threshold is the upper-limit index score. Students with index scores higher than this upper threshold are placed in the "presumptive admit" category.

Admission personnel then go over the applications in each presumptive category, looking for strengths and weaknesses that may not be captured by mere index scoring. Some applications will be moved down from the presumptive admit category to the discretionary admission group. Others will be moved up from presumptive denial. There are many things that can trigger such movement, including major, grade patterns, history of poor performance on standardized testing, personal characteristics, and so forth. Usually, though, the number of applications moved up or down is not very large.

At this point, those applications that are placed neither in the presumptive admit category nor the presumptive denial category (the vast majority of applications) are bundled in groups of twenty or thirty and circulated to admission committee members. At each school, some voting system is devised where admission committee members may use a limited number of votes to support applicants from each bundle. Those applicants who garner a prescribed minimum number of votes are offered admission.

The index score is a way of rank ordering the entire applicant pool. This is just the beginning of the evaluation of each applicant, but it is an important beginning.

GPA

GPA is actually a very slippery thing to evaluate. A number of problems may arise when trying to get a bead on the academic abilities of a particular applicant.

Grade Trends

The first problem is trying to "norm" the applicant—trying to find out from the record what is the applicant's best demonstrated work. What if a student has a 1.8 GPA for the first 40 units of college work and a 4.0 GPA the rest of the way out? Should this person be treated as a 3.3 GPA, the average over the college career, or as a 4.0? The high marks came later in the college career and occurred in the hardest courses—those at the upper-division level. If an admission committee member thinks that the entering class should be made up of students of the greatest demonstrated raw talent, then she is likely to dismiss the grades for the first 40 units. If she thinks this is unfair to other applicants, or that ethics require that the whole college career be considered, she may be forced to reject a very talented prospect.

How does the admission committee member compare our hypothetical student with a student who has exactly the same GPA but has had a 3.3 GPA every semester of her college career? Are these two 3.3 GPAs alike, or does one demonstrate greater talent? Does one demonstrate greater maturity and responsibility?

You can see that evaluation of an applicant's GPA can quickly become mired in collateral considerations. Of course, the index score for each applicant is a function of overall GPA and does not take into account grade improvement, breaks in time and then return to school, and so forth. Generally speaking, though, marked improvement in GPA over earlier semesters will cause committees to discount the earlier, poorer work. Likewise, if there is a significant time lag between an era of poor work that is followed by very good work upon return, committees are inclined to look most seriously at the work the applicant has done since her return to school.

GPA Translation

The second problem is found in how to determine what a GPA means relative to some pool of reference. Does a 3.8 from school X indicate a top student, or is grade inflation at school X so high that this GPA is about average? If the applicant is about the average for this school, then how does a committee screen out the effects of grade inflation and get to an appreciation of the applicants abilities? After all, under such a regime, a couple of bad grades could put a superior student behind the class average.

Maybe the problem is reversed, and the applicant's 3.1 GPA puts her in the top 10 percent of her graduating class. How will the admission committee know this information, and how should they adjust the index score of the applicant, if at all, if they do know about it? Of course, GPA translation is even more complicated than these simple examples suggest, since there is often great disparity within the same university across colleges and even departments. The top graduate of a school of engineering may have a 3.6 GPA, and the average for the college may be a 2.9 GPA, while just across campus the top graduate in liberal arts is always someone with a 4.0 GPA, and the student average is a 3.2 GPA.

Of course, where it increases the chance of admission, the applicant should supply as much information as possible to law schools about GPA, class standing, relative rankings, and the like.

The Unfamiliarity Problem

Law schools learn how to cope with grade norming and GPA translatability problems for most of their applicants because there is a track record of previous applicants from the same schools, and admission committee members can see how applicants from certain schools did in their past law school classes. For example, the University of Minnesota School of Law, a venerable and great institution, will have information on most major state schools and prominent private schools. Nevertheless, there are many schools that have never sent a graduate on to a particular law school, and that law school will have no way to evaluate the applicant in terms of school-track-record history.

> **Law schools are conservative in their admission practices, and the applicant from an unfamiliar institution will have an added burden not shared by applicants from institutions familiar to the law school.**

Law schools are conservative in their admission practices, and the applicant from an unfamiliar institution will have an added burden not shared by applicants from institutions familiar to the law school. If you apply to the University of Minnesota from UCLA, the University of Nebraska, or Duke, you will most likely be one in a long string of applicants to Minnesota from your school. But if you are from a small liberal arts school that has had only one, two, or perhaps even no applicants to Minnesota over the years, you should consider taking action to help the admission committee at the University of Minnesota understand your GPA and class grades. If your school supplies information such as average GPA by major, GPA ranges by major, or best of all, your class rank, then providing the information works in your favor. Make sure it is related to each school to which you apply. Even if your school has an established track record of students applying to many law schools, go ahead and include your class rank or other information if it makes your application appear more favorable. If your school does not publish such information, go to your prelaw adviser and ask for help in getting the policy changed or in getting the information especially for you on this occasion.

CURRICULUM

Major and Minor

Admission committees pay close attention to the majors and minors of their applicants. Some majors can hurt the applicant. For example, majors that are not considered particularly rigorous can be fatal, especially at the more competitive law schools (see Chapter 1 for a more complete discussion on this matter). An applicant can cure this problem by having a very demanding minor or by providing convincing information that the major did indeed require a demanding track of courses and work. For the most part, education, kinesiology, communication, and criminal justice majors are held to be somewhat suspect and can cause schools to actually reduce your index score.

On the other hand, majors that are universally held to be rigorous, such as physics, philosophy, engineering, life sciences, English, and so forth, may be rewarded with a boost in the index score, or at least a tacit boost in the minds of admission committee members. If you find yourself in a suspect major, read Chapter 1 and take appropriate action as suggested; also, of course, consult your prelaw adviser.

Course Load

Schools also pay attention to how long it took an applicant to complete a curriculum of classes and how courses are distributed during that time. For example, a person who did not work at all and took about 6 units per semester may be thought of differently than the person who averaged 15 units a semester, worked 20 hours a week, and is a single parent. Law school requires students to juggle a lot of things at once, and any evidence that a student can easily meet this requirement will aid in the admission decision.

Difficulty of Classes

To the extent that it makes itself obvious, a student who deliberately pursues a less rigorous course path will be thought less of than a student who takes the normal path or one that presents more difficulties. Sometimes, schools have information on specific courses at particular schools and can detect an applicant who takes a large helping of "gut" classes. Conversely, if a student takes an obviously difficult collection of courses, this will work to the applicant's favor.

Honors Classes and Exceptional Academic Achievement

Law schools also look for students who constantly challenge themselves or increase their course difficulty as they progress through their undergraduate careers. On this score, schools look for students who take honors classes or other courses that require substantially more work than is called for by the average class. Sometimes, honors courses may require substantial amounts of writing and analysis far beyond what is normally expected of similarly situated students in another, non-honors course. Make sure that the schools you apply to are made aware of any honors courses you took. If you have been recognized for exceptional academic achievement, make sure that information is also made available to the law schools you have applied to.

LSAT

Most members on law school admission committees are loathe to tinker around with LSAT scores for particular applicants, except in a couple of cases. You are pretty much stuck with your score if it is a bad one, and most efforts to explain it away or reduce its importance will fail. Nevertheless there are three situations where committees may engage in some interpretation of an LSAT score.

Score Relative to Members of Your Group and Special Consideration

If you are a member of a favored minority group, your LSAT score may be compared not against the entire applicant pool but against other applicants of either your specific minority group or against the groups of all favored minority applicants. This makes admission for members of these groups idiosyncratic because it depends upon an applicant's numbers compared to a relatively small pool. Because of the unpredictability of the pool size, the index scores tend to be very volatile from year to year. This is why applicants who are members of favored minority groups need to apply to more schools than other applicants and especially to schools that seem out of their range. More information on this point is available later in this chapter.

Sometimes, applicants who are much older than the rest of the pool may receive favorable consideration beyond what their LSAT score would dictate, since there is a lot of evidence that the LSAT scores of older test takers are substantially lower than those of younger test takers. Schools that take this information into account are rather enlightened, for most schools do not consider differences in LSAT performance based on age, and they surely do not compare LSAT scores across age populations.

Experience can enhance or discount an applicant's LSAT score and the weight of influence it normally has on the admission process. For example, if you were formerly captain of a nuclear attack submarine, there may be a consensus that your poor LSAT score is not to be given its normal weight. Also, if you have overcome extreme poverty or a troubled family life, a poor LSAT performance may be discounted. Please see Chapter 1 for more on these points.

> **Experience can enhance or discount an applicant's LSAT score and the weight of influence it normally has on the admission process.**

Number of Times You Have Taken the Exam

Law schools take into account the number of times you take the LSAT. There are several options schools may employ when evaluating applicants with multiple LSAT scores. First, schools can use your first score and ignore the others, perhaps on the theory that using the first score is more fair to the rest of the applicants in the pool who generally have but one score to offer. Second, schools may use your lowest score, maintaining a conservative approach to admission. Third, they may take your highest score, applying an optimistic approach to admission decisions.

In fact, what the vast majority of schools take, and what the LSDAS puts on its reports, is the average of your scores. It turns out, according the LSAC, that people who take the LSAT more than once generally improve by an average of two points on their second administration. Before you decide to take the test more than once, you should consider the following:

- First, most of the people retaking the test are probably doing so because there is a significant disparity between their practice scores and the score they received on their first official administration. In these cases, there is bound to be average improvement; the group will score better the second time because their first administration scores represent the trough of their abilities.

- Second, if you come in at the average, and therefore improve your test score by two points, after it is averaged it amounts to a one-point improvement. A one-point difference will have virtually no effect on admission decisions. You should take the attitude that you will take the test once and only once. See Chapter 2 for more information on this subject.

Explanations for Poor Performance

Sometimes, schools will entertain explanations for poor performance on the LSAT. Usually, such explanations take the form of claims that the applicant does not do well on standardized tests and that this poor performance has not been an indicator of the applicant's ability to succeed academically. In other words, the applicant did poorly on the SAT or ACT but did very well in undergraduate school.

There is no way of knowing how much effect these arguments have, but they probably do not have much influence. There may be exceptional cases that require careful consideration, but these are probably rare. This does not mean that if you have a history of poor standardized test performance and you nevertheless have performed well academically that you can just give up and make no attempt to argue the point. If you can make the argument, do so.

Disparity between GPA and LSAT

Occasionally, schools may listen to arguments that attempt to discount the LSAT by relying on an extremely strong GPA. If an applicant has a 4.0 GPA and scores a 135 on the LSAT, perhaps the LSAT score is not a reliable indicator of the applicant's ability to succeed. After all, the test does not measure motivation, persistence, work ethic, or, in short, what is usually termed "heart."

On these occasions, though, it seems difficult to get schools to bend very far. The LSAT has such hegemony over the admission process that it is very difficult to get committees to discount or overlook a bad score based on a good

GPA. The argument from the law school side is that the GPA of an applicant is *already* taken into account in the index score and that to make further allowances based on GPA would be to give it double weight in the process. However, if you find yourself with a very high GPA and a low LSAT score, you must make the argument. You must use every weapon you have available.

LETTERS OF RECOMMENDATION

The impact of letters of recommendation can vary widely, but usually letters are more closely scrutinized when an applicant is on the bubble for admission at a particular school or if the applicant is in a favored minority group. A strong, well-written letter that attacks a few key points can be extremely effective in aiding the applicant.

Most schools ask that you indicate whether or not you waive your right to see the letters of recommendation after they have been submitted. Recommenders are notified of these decisions before they submit letters. You should waive all rights to see your letters of recommendation. If you do not waive your rights in this matter, schools will assume the letter is not as forthcoming as it would be if the recommender were assured that her comments would not be seen by the student. Some admission personnel have said that they put no stock in letters where there is not an accompanying waiver.

PERSONAL STATEMENT

The personal statement is often the most difficult obstacle for law school applicants to get past. Applications frequently have been held up for months, lacking only a personal statement. You should have the final draft of your personal statement done during the summer before the fall semester of the year in which you are applying to law school. In Chapter 3, we discussed how to approach the personal statement, but the applicant should know that the personal statement really means very little in the evaluation process.

Rarely does a personal statement have a significant effect on the ultimate disposition of an applicant. Nevertheless, there is also a move toward paying more attention to these statements in an effort to get a feel for the candidate, especially for applicants who are members of favored minority groups and applicants with unusual backgrounds and experiences. If you are a favored minority applicant or you have had unusual experiences, as discussed in the next section, you must take great care with your personal statement, as it is likely to receive more scrutiny than those of other applicants.

> **All applicants must take reasonable care with their personal statements because, even if they may not prove to be of great help, a bad statement can be very damaging.**

All applicants, for this matter, must take reasonable care with their personal statements because, even if they may not prove to be of great help, a bad statement can be very damaging. A statement full of grammatical errors, slang, unusual syntax, and imprecise statements can be fatal to the applicant. Remember, *every* school you apply to is going to see the same personal statement, so a bad one affects all of your applications.

QUALIFYING FOR SPECIAL CONSIDERATION

There are generally two classes of applicants who qualify for special consideration or for greater contemplation on what sorts of qualities applicants can bring to the law school.

Admission or rejection of applicants from these classes may be idiosyncratic, meaning that admission committees may make decisions based on features more subjective than index scores or separate GPA and LSAT scores.

The problem for applicants who have nontraditional backgrounds or extraordinary experiences is that no one will say whether these applicants are being considered against the standard applicant pool, as is almost everyone else who applied, or if they are being considered against a much smaller pool of those people who will bring significant diversity to the law school class. At one school, an applicant may be considered so unusual as to receive extra consideration, while at another school, the applicant is lumped in with the mass of other applicants and has to fight it out per normal. This is why applicants who have unusual backgrounds and nontraditional students should increase the number of upper-end schools to which they apply. Please see Chapter 5 for more discussion on this point.

Nontraditional Backgrounds and Survival of Poverty and Abuse

If you have been a professional athlete, climbed some of the world's most difficult rock formations or highest mountains, commanded an aircraft carrier, swum the English Channel, saved a stranger from serious crime, or survived crushing poverty, an abusive childhood, or a violent spouse, law schools want to know the specifics of these backgrounds because they wish to assemble diverse classes with people who have a myriad of experiences.

If you have something unusual in your background of the types mentioned here, then make sure to bring that background to the attention of the law schools. Often, schools ask about these sorts of things in the application proper, though you will probably have to convey such information in your personal statement. If your background, experiences, or escape from poverty or abuse is dramatic enough, it may cause a school to ignore a substandard LSAT score or a mediocre GPA.

Favored Ethnicities

Members of favored ethnic groups are often not evaluated against the rest of the applicant pool. The excerpt from *Hopwood* v. *Texas* in Appendix B indicates that schools often adopt separate standards of admission for applicants who are members of favored minority groups. Just who do I mean when I say "favored minority applicants"? Generally, the term includes African Americans, Mexican Americans, Native Americans, and sometimes Hispanics who are not Mexican American. Who is favored can vary from school to school.

If you are a member of a favored group, your chances for admission to many law school programs will dramatically increase. If you are in a favored ethnic group, you must increase the number of applications in your level-one and level-two categories. See Chapter 5 for more discussion of this issue.

SERVICE AND ACCOMPLISHMENTS

A strong record of service activity or community accomplishment can be a significant factor in your packet. Usually, though, service will not exercise a large influence on your admissibility to more competitive law schools. If, for example,

You should only undertake service work if it is natural for you to do so, and the commitment comes from your heart.

service apparently came at the expense of your GPA, your volunteer work will do you no good at all. On the other hand, if you maintain a good GPA and have a strong service record, it works to impart the image of a person who is well organized and dedicated to community. However, please read the discussion in Chapter 1 before you rush off to augment your record with charity work. You should only undertake service work if it is natural for you to do so, and the commitment comes from your heart. Do not pursue service work merely to increase your admissibility into law school. The reward received compared to the work involved is precious little.

FAMILY MEMBERS WHO ARE ALUMNI

If you have a family member who is an alumnus of a school to which you are applying, then you should ask the person to contact his alma mater on your behalf. Sometimes, this can have a strong impact on your application packet. Many private schools also may ask on the application whether any family members have graduated from their school. Some private schools set aside "dynastic" positions in an entering class for relatives and children of alumni.

Applying to Law School

THE LAW SCHOOL CASTE SYSTEM

The most wretched and pernicious feature of the law school applications process is the excessive concern with law school rankings. To put it bluntly, law school rankings are a bunch of bunk. You would do best to avoid paying much attention to them and, instead, to concentrate more on substantive features of the schools you are applying to and how you will decide which offer of admission to accept. The desire for knowing the best of anything is deeply ingrained in American habit. We want to know the bottom line, who is the winner, and so forth. This is an unfortunate hangover of scientism, of the belief that subjective evaluation can be reduced to empirical observation. What is the "best" law school will vary with the idiosyncratic priorities, needs, desires, and sensibilities of each applicant. Certain important features in determining a best law school *are* subject to verification. Information, such as starting salary, bar passage rate, job placement data, and even the cachet of a law school, is important and quantifiable. However, this information is a beginning point in the evaluation of schools, not an end point. That is the main problem with surveys such as the one conducted by *U.S. News & World Report*. Information that should be treated as preliminary to an investigation all too often is used to supply an ultimate answer. The *U.S. News & World Report* rankings are sometimes just silly. People who

Chapter 5

make a lot of money actually spend time determining why school X is number thirty-one rather than tying with school Y for the thirtieth position. If we want to accuse our society of decadence, we should look not only to the excesses of youth, wealth, and privilege, but also to the excesses that come out of our desire for certainty. So long as applicants are led to believe that the rankings mean something, the schools will be in a very tough position and will be almost helpless to oppose this vicious practice.

You must not consider law schools in rank order. However, you should apply some objective criteria in evaluating whether or not to apply to or attend a particular law school. Generally, it is best to consider *groups* of law schools, rather than law schools separately. Application to law school is a game of probabilities, so you must concentrate on groups of law schools that are linked by similar admission rates, practices, job placement power, starting salary, and bar passage rates.

We break down law schools into four groups. Keep in mind that the borders of these groups overlap, and schools will often seem to fit equally well in two groups. Division among the groups is generally based on effective hiring area at law schools. This is a guideline, not a criterion; effective hiring area is often affected by the qualities and actions of individual graduates. The same sort of idiosyncratic qualities that go into admission decisions also affect a person's hireability. When sorting schools into one of the four groups though, I mostly look at *average* hireability. Some schools have an effective hiring area coextensive with the area of the U.S., whereas other schools have a very limited effective hiring area that may be no larger than the school's immediate location. Again, the effective hiring area of a school may be no obstacle to an individual with unique talents. The editor of a law review who is trilingual, regardless of her law school, will have a good chance at getting a job in any area the country.

National Schools

There is no doubt that there is a top group of law schools when measuring important verifiable data, such as starting salary, number of job offers per students, number of interviews on campus, and position of school graduates in middle career. This group is composed of relatively few schools that make up the truly "national" law schools—schools that have an effective hiring area roughly matching all of the United States. Approximately a dozen law schools have perennially been thought of as the most elite schools in the country. The list is somewhat flexible, but a defensible core list would include Harvard, Yale, Columbia, Stanford, the University of Chicago, the University of Virginia, Duke, the University of Michigan, Boalt Hall (Berkeley), New York University, the University of Pennsylvania, Cornell, and Northwestern. There is a lot of in-fighting among this group of schools, and occasionally there is some real movement in the so-called rankings. However, in terms of competitiveness, these schools usually remain pretty much as they have been year in and year out.

The average graduate from any of these schools can pretty much search for jobs nationwide and expect to get a good response in any market. The numbers required to gain admission to these schools are quite daunting. In the highest of the high, Yale, Stanford, and Harvard, a 3.9 GPA and a 95th percentile performance on the LSAT will not get you much notice. If it so desired, Yale could probably compose an entire class of 4.0 GPAs at the 99.8th percentile or above on the LSAT.

There is no doubt that there is a top group of law schools when measuring important verifiable data, such as starting salary, number of job offers per students, number of interviews on campus, and position of school graduates in middle career.

Further, most of these schools are connected to important, powerful families and political dynasties and are only too glad to maintain these connections. In disproportionate numbers, the leaders of our country, both in politics and business, are taken from these schools. There are important questions to be asked about why these schools are thought of the way they are. Is it because of their superior ability to train lawyers? Is it because they have the best teachers of law? The best facilities? The best environment in which to learn? The answers to at least some of these questions are arguably "no," depending on what the applicant wants from a law school. In a sense, these are the wrong questions because these schools are much more than training grounds for lawyers. Sometimes, it appears that law students merely provide some of these schools with an excuse to engage in other activities.

Much of the interest at these schools is not directed at the students but at much bigger targets, such as prestigious publications, establishing academic centers, pursuing relationships with other countries, and developing relationships with large corporate donors. I do not mean to make it sound as if the student is an afterthought at these schools, because the future prestige of the school largely hinges on the students it enrolls today. However, there is clearly much more going on than just teaching a group of people how to parse a set of facts in a case.

In a sense, this grand activity serves the student, since the student's degree of success after graduation is determined many times by the prestige of the school from which she graduates. All of these activities help keep the school at the top, and when the school is at the top, its graduates are at the top. As a law professor once remarked to me, "You [meaning me and the other students] are something I have to put up with when I'm not publishing articles, drawing consultation fees, or attending conferences." This professor was joking, but there is more truth in his statement than makes one comfortable.

Keep in mind that the number of schools that truly have a national market is relatively small. For example, last year, a former student returned to El Paso to work as a summer associate after his second year of law at a school ranked in the top twenty-five by *U.S. News & World Report.* He was somewhat bitter because his school's ranking had not helped him find jobs in Texas; employers just did not have enough experience with the school's graduates to feel comfortable risking a hire, and the cachet of the school was insufficient to overcome this reluctance. An applicant from Yale may also have been a novelty to a Texas firm, but Yale's perennial high esteem might have been sufficient to outweigh other concerns. In other words, the cachet of the top schools wears off rather quickly as one goes farther down the rankings.

This is another of the bad things that arises from efforts to rank schools: it misleads applicants into making incorrect judgments about a school's effective hiring area. Past a very short list of schools, firms often stick with entrenched hiring patterns because they have long-established relationships with area and local schools, know the professors and trust their evaluations of candidates, and have an extensive track record of hiring graduates from those schools and can make comparisons among applicants. Some firms seem to not even entertain the idea of hiring associates from national schools. Often, hires from national schools have different career goals and aspirations than graduates from other law schools that can run counter to what is best for the firm. For example, firms might accurately see national school graduates as more likely to job-hop and less likely to be committed to the firm than others might be, especially the farther the

Past a very short list of schools, firms often stick with entrenched hiring patterns because they have long-established relationships with area and local schools, know the professors and trust their evaluations of candidates, and have an extensive track record of hiring graduates from those schools and can make comparisons among applicants.

firm is from economic centers of power, such as New York, Los Angeles, and Chicago. To an eleven-member firm in Frankfort, Kentucky, an applicant who graduated from Harvard may have the added burden of convincing the firm that she really wants to come to that area of the country and will be a committed member of the firm. For small to medium-size firms, hirings can cause crucial shifts in work load and dedication of funds; therefore, the members want to be as certain as they can that the hire not only is well trained but also will develop a strong commitment to the firm. Even graduates of national schools confront difficulties in being hired based on regional biases.

Regional Schools

Regional institutions are schools that have strong reputations within some relatively large but limited geographic area. Southern Methodist University, the University of Minnesota, the University of Wisconsin, the University of Washington, the University of North Carolina, the University of Iowa, and Indiana University–Bloomington are examples. The power of these schools to place graduates probably eclipses or is equal to that of the national schools for a large area around the schools. Usually, these schools place 50–70 percent of their graduates in the state in which the school is located or within a radius of about 200 miles.

Regional schools generally enjoy strong hiring patterns in their areas, but the farther one gets from these schools, the weaker their placement ability becomes as they encroach on territory occupied by neighboring regional institutions. Regional schools are characterized by the following features. First, they are considered to be the premier law schools of their area. Second, other law schools in the area do not significantly impact the regional school's ability to place its candidates. Third, they are usually thought of as the regional law center. Fourth, more judges in the state, and perhaps surrounding states, are taken from this institution than from other law schools in the area. Fifth, the farther one travels from the school, the greater the power of the next neighboring regional school. For example, the University of Minnesota and the University of Wisconsin are both schools with rich legal histories and venerable traditions that deliver about the best training a student can hope to find. However, the hiring power of one diminishes significantly the closer it comes to the other. They each place about 65 percent of their graduates in their own states, but only a few graduates from Minnesota cross the state line to practice in Wisconsin each year and vice versa.

Subregional Schools

Subregional schools are those that are not considered to be the premier law school in their area and are not considered the region's primary legal resource. While it will probably have a number of graduates in the judiciary in the region, it will not be the dominant graduating law school for staffing judgeships. The fine law school at Wake Forest University is an example. Despite being surrounded by at least one national school, Duke, and a very strong regional school, the University of North Carolina, Wake Forest graduates place very similarly to those of strong regional schools. About 60 percent of its graduates stay in the state, about right for a regional school, but the school has an effective hiring area resembling that of a strong regional school rather than that of the kind of "local" school described below. In times of economic stress or tight markets in the area, graduates of the subregional school are likely to suffer before regional or national school graduates.

Local Schools

Graduates of local schools almost always have a much more difficult time finding jobs, and when they do, their pay is often much lower than that of their colleagues.

Localized institutions are schools that have a limited placement area. Sometimes, these schools can be dramatically hemmed in. This happens most frequently in the major urban areas. This can be compounded by close proximity to national or strong regional institutions. For example, look at schools located in Virginia or North Carolina that are not regional, subregional, or national schools. Within 250 miles are the University of Virginia, Duke, the University of North Carolina, Wake Forest, William and Mary, Washington and Lee, George Mason, George Washington, and American. This sort of competition makes it very difficult for a graduate of our hypothetical school to compete for jobs in the area. This can have the curious effect of graduates from these local institutions ultimately taking jobs far away in other states because of the highly competitive market into which they have graduated. Graduates of local schools almost always have a much more difficult time finding jobs, and when they do, their pay is often much lower than that of their colleagues.

On the other hand, the University of Wyoming School of Law is a "local" school by the guidelines employed here. While there is less need for lawyers in Wyoming and the interior Northwest than there is in the mid-Atlantic seaboard, the University of Wyoming is also the only game around. This means that its law students may get to know lawyers and area law firms in a way students from our hypothetical Virginia or North Carolina school cannot. This will be an important asset when interviewing for summer or permanent positions. When assessing possible local schools for application, get a feel for the hiring dynamics of the area in which it is located.

INFORMATION YOU SHOULD KNOW ABOUT THE SCHOOLS TO WHICH YOU APPLY

There is a wealth of statistical and other information that is generally available from every law school and university that you should obtain and study before submitting your application. I have divided this information into two types: career information and environmental information.

Career Information

All law schools keep very close track of how their graduates fare in the job market, the bar exam, and other matters. As a result of this tracking, each school has a wealth of information it can pass on to prospective students. You should take it as a bad sign if a school does not wish to have this information made public or declines to share it with you. The kind of information you should look for follows.

- Average number of job offers per graduating student

- Average starting salary of graduates

- Median starting salary of graduates

- Percentage of graduates employed six months after graduation

Each school has a wealth of information it can pass on to prospective students. You should take it as a bad sign if a school does not wish to have this information made public or declines to share it with you.

- Percentage of graduates ultimately employed in the legal field

- Percentage of graduates employed at firms (broken down by firm size and location), in government jobs, and so forth

- Number of students who won judicial clerkships

- Number of on-campus interviews by employers

- List of the most active interviewers on campus

- Percentage of graduates who stay in the state or the area, as well as the percentage of graduates who go to other states and the states where they go

- Graduates' satisfaction with the law school

- The bar-passage rate of graduates

- Midcareer graduate employment and salaries

- Summer employment data, including salaries, placement, and the percentage of students who split their summers (work the first half of summer at one job and the second half at another)

- Average school debt per graduate

- Availability of debt forgiveness programs and requirements of the programs

- Commitment of the placement office (some offices will only aid a graduate in job searches for a specified period of time)

Environmental Information

Aside from career information, you should also know a lot about the area surrounding the school, the economic environment, issues of safety, and so forth. After all, you will spend three years of your life in and around your law school, so you should be prepared to balance its "misery" or "delight" factor along with other data. The following incomplete list suggests some things you might want to ask about a law school and its surrounding area. Be fair, though, and make sure you subject all the schools you apply to to this kind of scrutiny, not just "suspect" schools. You may be surprised by what you find out about places you thought you knew or were familiar with.

- What sorts of crime have occurred on campus recently?

- What is the crime rate of the surrounding community?

- Do most of the houses in the area have burglar bars or obvious security devices?

- If you have children or are considering having children, does the school have an established day-care facility available to you?

- What is the cost of living for the area?

- Is there adequate parking to serve students at the law school?

- Does the school offer escorts for students walking to their vehicles or the bus stops at night?

- If you are married, does the school have student family housing? If a school does have such housing, what sort of shape is the housing in?

- What level of health coverage is available to students and their families and at what cost?

- Is the school aesthetically pleasing?

- How late is the library open?

- Are their enough study carrels in the library to make sure that each student can have one?

- Does each study carrel have access to the Internet?

- Is the law school set up well? Are library maps and stack directions easy to follow?

- If you are single, what are the dorms like?

- Are dormitories mixed between undergraduate and graduates?

- What recreational activities are sponsored by the law school?

HOW MANY SCHOOLS SHOULD YOU APPLY TO?

One of the worst mistakes a prospective law student can make is to apply to too few schools. I recommend that you apply to no less than twelve institutions. Under certain circumstances, students should apply to at least twenty schools. These circumstances are discussed below. If you apply to a dozen schools, you should divide these schools up into four groups. Three of the schools you apply to should be institutions where your chances of admission are slim. Obviously, what counts as "slim" depends on your numbers. If you have a 3.0 GPA and score in the 70th percentile on the LSAT, then the University of Texas at Austin, Duke, Cornell, Wisconsin, and Minnesota are all slim possibilities for admission. The second three schools should be institutions where you probably will not be admitted, but where you stand a 25 percent chance of getting in. The third set of three schools should be institutions where you stand a 50 percent chance or better of admission. Finally, you should have three schools where you stand a very high chance of admission. Many times I have seen students get boxed out—left without an offer of admission because they applied to too few schools or applied only to the top schools. Bear in mind that at schools such as Stanford, Yale, Harvard, Chicago, and Columbia, you cannot count on admission even if you have a 3.9 GPA and score above the 95th percentile on the LSAT. All applicants should apply to a range of schools. The LSAC's *Official Guide to U.S. Law Schools* contains admission grids for most schools broken down by GPA and LSAT score. You can use the information in these grids to estimate your chances of admission to a particular school, but please read the information on page 139 first.

One of the worst mistakes a prospective law student can make is to apply to too few schools. I recommend that you apply to no less than twelve institutions. Under certain circumstances, students should apply to at least twenty schools.

When to Apply to More Schools

There are three circumstances where I advise applicants to apply to up to twenty law schools. The first is when an applicant has extremely low numbers—for instance, a 2.5 GPA and a 30th percentile score on the LSAT. In this circumstance, the applicant should apply to fifteen schools that are considered to be in the bottom tier of law schools. Five applications should be directed at schools that are seemingly just beyond the applicant's reach. Remember, all

ABA–accredited law schools deliver a first-rate education, and whether or not you are a good lawyer often has little to do with grades or where you went to law school. Prospective clients do not ask F. Lee Bailey where he went to law school or what sort of grades he made.

The second circumstance that justifies a higher number of applications is when an applicant has very good numbers, but not quite good enough for top-tier institutions. If you are Caucasian and have a 3.5 GPA and score in the 80th percentile on the LSAT, you should make twelve applications to schools that seem just beyond your reach: Schools ranging in ranking from number five to twenty-five.

Applicants from ethnic minorities with favored admission status generally should apply to more than a dozen schools, especially if they have "mixed" or good but marginal numbers or numbers that are either fairly good or very bad. An example of the "mixed" category would be a student who has a 3.8 GPA but scores in the 40th percentile on the LSAT. She may want to still use the four category approach, but triple the normal number of applications for the first tier of schools where she perceives a slim chance of admission. This also goes for an applicant who is an ethnic minority favored for admission by law schools and has fairly good numbers— for example, a 3.4 GPA and scores in the 80th percentile on the LSAT. The reason applicants in these categories should increase the number of applications is because admission of ethnic minority applicants is often idiosyncratic and not measured against the standard applicant pool. Even if you have only a decent GPA and a good LSAT score, then, as a member of a minority group, you should consider tripling the number of schools you apply to in the two highest categories of your four-part set up. For example, if you have a 3.3 GPA and a 158 or above on the LSAT, then you should increase the number of applications to schools at which you think you have a slim or marginal chance of being accepted.

Applicants who are members of minority groups and have poor numbers still have a good shot at being accepted to law school. Keep the four-part set up and triple the number of schools in the bottom category.

Favored minority applicants are generally not competing against the entire applicant pool, but against other minority applicants. Since this pool is much smaller than the entire pool, it is unpredictable and dynamic in a way that larger pools are not. The average numbers of minority applicants to a particular school may vary widely from year to year. Because of this variance, you need to apply to more schools than when the pool is more stable. You should consider doubling the number of applications in the two highest categories of schools to which you are applying. This will increase the chances that you will apply to a school where your application will compete well with those of other minority applicants.

Likewise, if you have a decent GPA, for example a 3.0, but a weak LSAT, such as 144 and below, double or triple the number of schools you are applying to in the bottom two categories of your four-part setup. Also, if you find yourself in this situation, be realistic about where you apply. Your top category may not include any national schools and perhaps just one regional school, but make sure you read the next section on how to calculate chances of admission at a school.

> **Favored minority applicants are generally not competing against the entire applicant pool, but against other minority applicants. Since this pool is much smaller than the entire pool, it is unpredictable and dynamic in a way that larger pools are not.**

CALCULATING YOUR CHANCES OF ADMISSION

The Official Guide to U.S. Law Schools, which may be bought together with the LSACD or purchased alone, contains information on chances of admission to particular law schools based on GPA and LSAT score. Other published sources also provide this information, but that information is not as authoritative as that put out by the LSAC. If there is nothing in your application that sets you apart from other applicants, such as extensive work experience, minority status, veteran status, overcoming severe obstacles to education, and so forth, then take the odds calculated by the LSAC at face value. If you are a member of an ethnic minority group with favored admission status, then you should double, or even triple, the admission odds calculated for a particular school. Veterans with significant combat experience can also increase their odds to double or triple, as can those people who have held exceptional positions, such as a former attack submarine captain.

Average veterans and nonminorities who have overcome significant obstacles, such as poverty, can bump the odds somewhat, but not greatly. Nonminority applicants who have significant work experience or unusual backgrounds can expect a bit of a boost, but not a great one. Women applicants may get a very slight advantage, but not enough to factor in when looking at the odds at a particular school.

DECIDING WHICH OFFER TO ACCEPT

Deciding which offer of admission to accept is a relatively straightforward proposition, as long as you keep a few things in mind. One thing to remember is that you are not shopping for a piece of art. You don't buy what you like, or what feels good to you. You should select a law school based on practical considerations. One consideration, of course, might be the feel of the place, its aesthetic charm, and so forth. But this is only one factor to be considered. Other considerations include the reputation of the school, its success at placing graduates, starting salary of graduates, its effective area of placement, bar-passage rate, your assessment of the school's environment, and, if relevant, cost of attendance.

Remember that there is no such thing as a bad ABA–accredited law school. This is the truth. They are all high-quality institutions, and the training at Harvard will be little different from the training at the University of Idaho. Perhaps unfairly, though, much of your future hinges on where you go to law school.

Offers from National Schools

If you are lucky enough to have GPA and LSAT numbers that bring offers of admission from the elite dozen or so schools mentioned at the beginning of this chapter, then the decision which offer to accept is a personal and idiosyncratic one. Many advisers will say I am crazy not to advise people to go to Harvard or Yale over Virginia or NYU, and, not many years ago, I would have agreed with them. The truth is that graduates from any of the national schools will probably have multiple job offers, very high salaries, and good chances at judicial clerkships. There may be some slight loss of opportunity for selecting Penn over Harvard, for example, but this is arguable and certainly will not be the case generally. The only case in which it is probably terribly important to select the more prestigious school is if the applicant has already decided that she might want to teach in a law school. These cases will be rare, and even if a person decides prior to attending law school that she wants to teach in a law school, chances are she will not have the same feelings at the end of the process or even the qualifications to become a law school professor.

It is unlikely that an applicant can make a mistake in selecting within the same group. However, it likely would be a mistake, when the candidate is admitted to a national school, to elect to attend a regional, subregional, or local institution. This rule is fairly hard and fast, but there are a couple of situations that might justify a deviation. Say you were accepted at the University of Texas at Austin and Northwestern University and that you are a Texas resident. Even though Northwestern is in the elite group of schools, it is probably not sufficiently better thought of than Texas to justify the difference in expense. Here, you must make your decision based on likelihood. The high likelihood of getting a job offer as a graduate of Texas that is close to or matches a job offer that you would get coming out of Northwestern warrants sacrificing the little difference in reputation and effective hiring area.

A more interesting question arises when you have been accepted by Texas and Duke. Some might think this a close call, but I see it as rather simple. You go to Duke. There may be a $50,000 difference in educational expenses, but there is a strong likelihood that, if you attend Duke, the difference will be made up by higher starting salary or by greater marketability that lets you practice law wherever you want.

A few years ago, I advised a student who had been offered admission to the law schools at Richmond and the University of Virginia. She came to me and said that she thought she would go to Richmond because she liked the school better. We sat down and went through placement data, bar-passage-rate information, average starting salaries reported, student satisfaction surveys, and so forth. It became clear to her at some point that she was making her decision based on hard-to-justify subjective considerations. There is plenty to be said for how one feels about a school; after all, we often make decisions based on intuition. You must include your intuition along with the other data you look at to make a decision about which school to attend, but do not allow your undefined feelings to operate as a trump to all other data you can collect about a particular school. On your evaluation list, make a place for your overall feeling about a school and use it as just one criterion of evaluation.

In actuality, the best lawyers I have ever known have not come from the prestigious schools. The best attorney I know came from a poorly ranked law school, and she barely avoided failing. Performance as a lawyer does not owe a whole lot to where one went to school. However, we do not live in a very well-functioning meritocracy, so the best in any field may not be the most highly rewarded. This is the case with law. The average graduate of an average law school will never recoup the disparity in earnings and offers that his Yale counterpart will have.

Despite the similarity in training across schools, there are some very good reasons to go to the upper tier of law schools if you can gain admission. First, you will make more money if you wish. I say "if you wish" because many graduates from these schools go into government service, clerk for judges, go on to doctoral programs, or enter public service law. If you choose to go into private practice, though, the difference in salary between a graduate from a national school and a graduate from a strong regional school can be quite high.

> **There is plenty to be said for how one feels about a school; after all, we often make decisions based on intuition. You must include your intuition along with the other data you look at to make a decision about which school to attend, but do not allow your undefined feelings to operate as a trump to all other data you can collect about a particular school.**

Second, you will be able to shop your application around nationwide. You will not be necessarily tied to one area of the country. There will always be the sentiment that it looks better on the firm's letterhead and office directory to have the Duke J.D. rather than the Nebraska J.D.

Third, a national school graduate is likely to receive multiple job offers. Most law students around the country will be scrambling to find summer employment or to get an offer from a firm, but the Yale graduate does not have to go through this. Instead, thousands of employers come to New Haven to fete the students and try to lure them off to Anchorage or St. Louis. This is especially nice when the market is sluggish. Graduates from national schools never have a hard time finding work, no matter what shape the legal market is in.

Fourth, if your goal is to be a judge or to hold some other political office, it helps to be from a big-name school or, at least, the dominant regional school in your location.

> **By going to a school like Harvard, you will be connected to people of power for the rest of your life. When people are in a position to throw opportunity in someone's direction, they usually look to their friends.**

Fifth, by going to a school like Harvard, you will be connected to people of power for the rest of your life. Your classmates, and perhaps even you, will go on to high government and business positions. When people are in a position to throw opportunity in someone's direction, they usually look to their friends. The bottom line is that if you can gain admission to one of these elite schools, then go.

The people admitted to these schools are few relative to the rest of the law school market, and in many cases admission to these schools is a matter of luck. If you do not get into one of these schools, don't worry. I have no regrets at all about attending Virginia Law, and I thoroughly enjoyed it, though, looking back, I do not understand why they decided to offer me admission. I love the professors there, and the environment is unmatchable in my view. But I also know that

I did not need to go there to do what I ended up doing—teaching undergraduate and graduate students political science. I am confident that anyone can attain their goals without attending a national law school.

Offers from Regional Schools

If you do not get any offers from national schools, then your best bet is to go to a regional school with a strong placement record and average starting salary and bar-passage rate. You need to exercise some care in which school you select because you will probably end up practicing law in the state or area where the school is located. You want to make sure that you go to school in a region you won't mind living in on an indefinite basis.

If you can, I recommend that you visit your two best options and try to get a feel for the area and the way the law school operates. Talk to law students and ask the placement office for detailed information.

Just because you attend a regional school does not mean that you cannot get a job out of the school's region; it just means that the odds are more strongly against it compared to applicants from national institutions. But if you are editor of the law review, no matter where you go to school, you will have opportunities all over the United States. Even if you go to a regional school, superior performance can make you sell like a graduate from a national institution.

Offers from Subregional Schools

These schools often have effective placement areas similar to the dominant regional school in the area but are much more affected by fluctuations in demand and other market influences that the regional school generally resists. There tends

There tends to be a lot of rivalry between regional and subregional schools.

to be a lot of rivalry between regional and subregional schools. The main differences are generally expressed in starting salaries and opportunities for positions such as clerkships, and, later, in judgeships. Often, firms will be loyal to one subregional school over another and rarely hire new attorneys from other schools. In an area with many subregional schools, the attendant rivalries can be quite impressive.

If it looks like you will attend a subregional school, take the time to visit your top choices. Perhaps, unlike with national and regional schools, you might wish to talk to area attorneys about hiring patterns, difficulties faced immediately following graduation, and so forth.

Offers from Local Schools

By "local," I mean schools that have a very limited placement area for graduates. If you do not have offers from national, regional, or subregional schools, then where you choose to go to law school becomes even more important than for the person trying to select from regional and subregional institutions. As with regional and subregional choices, visit your top offers, ask questions of students, and obtain objective career information about graduates.

Again, just because you have to go to a local institution does not mean that you cannot get a job across the country practicing law; it simply means that it is much less likely to occur than if you go to a regional or national institution. As mentioned previously for regional schools, superior performance can make up for a lot of the difference in marketability between the three divisions made here.

Determining Where a School Belongs

As with most classificatory schemes, the difficult decisions are found around the edges of the classification. I used to have a more expansive list of which schools counted as "national" for effective hiring, but this list has shrunk considerably. The reason for this is that student after student from schools ranked in the twenties, high teens, and even middle teens have reported behavior on the part of interviewing law firms that is more indicative of the sort encountered by graduates of regional institutions. For example, recently a former student from a school ranked in the high teens tried to interview for jobs in El Paso, and even though he was an El Paso resident, he had rather stiff competition from Texas Tech and University of New Mexico applicants. He was asked questions such as how the firm could be sure that he really wants to live in El Paso. If he had not been a lifelong El Paso resident, it is easy to imagine that he would not have even received interviews with the El Paso firms. This is just a single example, but once one gets past the group of historically elite schools, there is a lot of evidence that rank means little.

I still would generally say that an applicant admitted to a national school who decides to attend a school outside this list is usually making a mistake, unless the school attended is a strong regional school and the applicant has specific, convincing reasons for making the decision. Of course, this is not *always* the case, but showing such a decision to be rational under evaluation of factors that matter would be rather difficult.

Except for grouping schools as national, regional, subregional, and local, you should avoid all other schemes to rank or prioritize schools. Especially avoid ranking schools within a group. You can and should decide which school is best for you with information that is readily available and taking into consideration factors that are most important to you.

Paying for Law School

Chapter 6

All applicants have concerns about how they will be able to pay for law school. Do not worry about this aspect very much during the application process. If you are admitted to a law school, then one way or another, it will make sure you can pay the bill. For example, if attendance at a school and living costs exceed the maximum amount of loans available, do not assume that you will be required to come up with the difference from private funds. If that were the case, then only the very rich could attend many law schools. In fact, few people who attend law school have any serious financial wherewithal. Beware, though, that if you must rely on a combination of private as well as public sources of funding, private sources will check your credit background. Even if you have bad credit, it does not mean that you are not a good credit risk for law school debt. It means that you may have to shop around a bit more and work closely with the financial aid office of the school you attend.

Almost everyone in law school receives financial aid. Law schools have at their disposal a complicated array of means to help students pay their tuition. Some schools run their own loan programs, making up any difference in need in a student package from special funds made available to the school. Other special loan programs are also in place to make up shortfalls of federal and state programs. Do not worry. The schools will do almost all of the work in this area and present you with a package that will cover your tuition and living expenses.

COST-BENEFIT CONSIDERATIONS

Law school is obviously very expensive, and you should certainly make cost considerations part of your decision-making process. But you should be cautioned against being overly concerned with costs. Often, people shy away from what appears to them, at the moment, to be a tremendous amount of debt. Contemplation of debt of $75,000 or $100,000 in school loans can be absolutely debilitating to some people. However, let me try to keep you from dwelling on the debt, because I have seen many students make poor decisions on where to attend law school out of fear of taking on debt.

The amount of debt you incur going to law school is almost always well spent in the sense that your salary will handle the debt far better than you imagine. You must not think about how you make and spend money now, but how you will make and spend money when you graduate from law school and take on a job in the legal world. Suppose, for example, you can attend a school in your state that is a subregional or local school, is very inexpensive, and may result in you leaving school with no debt or a very small amount of debt. Suppose further that you are accepted by a couple of strong out-of-state regional schools. Chances are that you will be making a mistake if you shy away from going to an out-of-state regional school merely to avoid debt. The difference in starting salary will probably be approximately $20,000 per year or more. In addition, you may even find yourself without a job for some period of time after graduating from the less expensive school.

To make this point a bit more real, suppose you are accepted at Texas Tech University School of Law, a very good program with one of the most exciting deans in the country. Suppose you are also admitted to the University of North Carolina, a very strong regional school. As a resident of Texas, attending Texas Tech will be very cheap. Even if you go $60,000 into debt attending North Carolina, at a cost of around $15,000 a year, it will still be much cheaper for you to go to North Carolina than to Texas Tech. First, the difference in median starting salary favors North Carolina by $11,000 per year. Pay raises early in the careers of graduates of these schools will just exacerbate this difference. When you consider that 99 percent of North Carolina graduates have found permanent work six months after graduation, as opposed to 77 percent for Texas Tech, you can see that the tuition premium in going to North Carolina is money well spent. Further, the North Carolina student is much likelier to receive good summer employment, ranging between $1,000 and $1,800 a week in private firms, and can reduce the cost of law school more appreciably than can the Texas Tech student.

Do not get me wrong, I am not making any kind of judgment about Texas Tech or North Carolina. Texas Tech is a very good school, but in order to select Texas Tech over North Carolina, you are going to have to have something more compelling than tuition differential. The point is, do your homework; do not focus on the amount of money you will have to borrow, but rather pay attention to what that money will buy you. In the case of North Carolina, your money buys you a higher starting salary and a greater effective area of hire. Over the course of time, it is likely that the North Carolina graduate will far outstrip the Texas Tech graduate in terms of earned income. Often, the more expensive school is the best buy; do not use differential in tuition costs as an important reason to select one school over another.

APPLYING FOR FINANCIAL AID

When to Start the Paperwork

You may recall that some law schools do not send out admission offers until late spring, and if you are on a waiting list for a school, you may not know whether or not you are admitted until the first week of school. Clearly, you cannot wait to see which school you are attending before starting the financial aid process.

You cannot wait to see which school you are attending before starting the financial aid process.

Some students overlook the fact that their ultimate financial aid package depends upon their tax filings for the previous year and on the information contained in the Free Application for Federal Student Aid (FAFSA). Virtually all financial aid in law school is calculated on the basis of need. Schools and the federal agencies that are charged with calculating your need use your previous year's tax return and information that you self-report on the FAFSA. Since these two items comprise the lynch pin for the whole process, you must have these things out of the way as soon as possible. For example, file your tax return as soon as you receive all of your W-2s, 1099s, and so forth. The sooner you get this out of the way the better.

The FAFSA may be filled out, as well as electronically signed, on line (http://www.fafsa.ed.gov). Alternatively, you may pick up a hard copy of the form from your undergraduate school or any law school. I recently worked through the online option and found it to be very friendly and easy to use. Be careful that you choose to fill out the correct form, since multiple years of the form are available at the same time. For example, I worked through the online option of the form on December 6, 1999, and had the choice of filling out the form for the 1999–2000 school year or the 2000–2001 school year. Remember, you will be filling the form out for the *upcoming* year. That is, if you are a senior applying to school for admission in fall 2000, fill out the 2000–2001 form. As with your tax return, fill out this form as soon as possible. Many students applying to law school are still dependents of their parents for tax purposes. This means that these students may need to file a copy of their parents' tax return, as well as their own, when applying for financial aid at the school they ultimately attend. Graduate students are considered independent of their parents in determining aid and loan eligibility under federal programs. Nevertheless, some law school want to know more detailed information about where students' financial support comes from and will ask for your parents' tax return. If you need to file your parents' tax return with your financial aid paperwork, make sure that you let your parents know early.

Each law school makes its own determinations concerning loan eligibility and so forth. What financial aid you are eligible for is determined by cost of attendance, including tuition, books, rent, food, and health insurance, and financial resources that the student currently has or expects in the upcoming academic year. Bear in mind that adjustment may be made for extraordinary circumstances; for example, a student may have a large preexisting debt that may cause a change in the student's need formula.

Once you know which law school you will be attending, you can start the federal loan paperwork. If you have problems understanding or obtaining federal loan paperwork, the financial aid office at your future school should be glad to help.

SUMMER EMPLOYMENT

If you are a bit of an adventurer, look for work internationally.

Most first-year law students are so focused on their studies that they cannot even think about summer employment until after the fall semester is over. Indeed, you probably will not even be allowed to interview with potential employers until January of your first year, at the earliest. Therefore, finding summer employment after your first year is a bit of a scramble, and sometimes students have very difficult times getting jobs in sectors or areas that they desire. Remember that there are a lot of places to gain employment as a law student; most governmental agencies, both state and federal, have many positions for law students. These positions do not pay nearly as well as private-sector employment (usually 50 percent, or even less, of what you would get at a firm), but the work can be very interesting. Your placement office will have a lot of information concerning summer employment, so it is not necessary here to go over all of the aspects of finding a summer job.

Nevertheless, there are some things to keep in mind that may prove helpful when you look for a summer position. First, people often do not consider this, but contemplate the possibility of going overseas. There are many law offices around the world that are owned and operated by American law firms. These offices also need summer associates and try to hire for their needs, as do offices in the United States. In addition, sometimes it is quite a difficult for personnel at these offices to advertise their summer positions and to make contact with potential summer hires. There is more work involved, and the firms are very busy—sometimes they too are caught scrambling at the last minute. This can give you an opportunity. Go through the Internet or another medium to locate law offices overseas, and then make inquiries. In addition, a lot of potential summer hires are probably scared off by traveling so far for summer work and by having to live in another country. No doubt there are attendant problems in going to many places. How does a person working for ten weeks in Hong Kong find a place to live? These problems may have already been resolved by the firm, so if you are a bit of an adventurer, look for work internationally.

Second, students are generally unaware that virtually every law professor can hire summer help for research. Most schools make funds available to professors for summer researchers. Sometimes professors advertise this fact, but many times they do not. As a hedge against possible summer limbo, approach a professor you like and admire and ask about summer research. Do this early, perhaps even as early as November of your first year. If you end up getting a job with the private sector for the summer, any professor will forgive you for canceling out on the research job. If your first choices in professors do not have anything available, are using other students, or just will not hire first-year students, then broaden your search and approach professors you do not know. Be aware that the money for this sort of work is awful, but at least it is something. In addition, you may get a real taste of research by working on important or interesting topics. You may help a professor with an article, or you may even help to prepare a case for litigation or help the professor consulting on a case.

Third, do not be too proud to walk around the legal district in the city where you attend law school; go into firms, introduce yourself, drop off your resume, and generally sell yourself. The bigger firms will not pay much attention to you, but you can give them a shot anyway. You may find a job with a smaller firm that finds itself swamped and can use some competent help. Again, the pay will not be great, but the experience and the connections made can be invaluable.

Fourth, placement offices are indispensable, but they do not have a monopoly on information; go to your professors and ask them if they have any ideas about where you can find summer work. Some may throw you out of the office, while others may draw you a map to the placement service center, but a couple may say "As a matter of fact . . ." However you go about getting summer employment, do not be shy. Ask anyone and everyone for their opinion and if they have heard of any particular jobs that sound good. Also, do not think that anything is beneath your dignity. A friend once spent a summer working for a docketing clerk of a court, a job which she thought was going to be tedious and mind numbing. She actually learned a tremendous amount, especially about how to accomplish filings in the jurisdiction, and made new friends and some important connections.

Your First Semester

Chapter 7

Preparation for law school must begin long before classes start. Law school does not begin slowly; there is no acclimating period. From the first day, study requirements and expectations of students are set at a very high level. You will have assigned reading for the first day of class, and, if your experience is anything like mine, the instructor simply will come in and without pause start grilling students at random about the day's reading. In many law schools, there is a bulletin board where first-day assignments are posted. Make sure you get off to a good start; do your reading. You probably have not yet learned how to "read" a case, so you can expect to be lost and intimidated in your first classes. I remember several times at the beginning of my first year asking myself, "Is the instructor talking about the same case that I read last night?" Often, it seemed as if what I was supposed to get out of a case and what I actually got out of a case were hopelessly irreconcilable. After a few weeks, though, you begin to get the hang of reading cases, and things start coming into focus. The important thing is not to panic or come to the conclusion that you just can't make it. You can and will make it.

Law school not only is mentally demanding but also constitutes an onslaught on the mind and the body. In a matter of a few short hours after the beginning of classes, it is easy to feel completely overwhelmed. Therefore, your attention and energy must be focused on trying to cope with this new environment. This means that you should make sure that your life is as settled as it possibly can be when you begin school.

BEFORE CLASS BEGINS

Before you begin law school, there are a number of things you can do to make your first semester easier. If you are a naturally disorganized person, you must do your best to change your ways.

Do not arrive in town the day before classes or orientation are scheduled to begin. Try to arrive the last week in July or the first week in August to nail down your living quarters. Make sure you understand the setting of your quarters. Find out who your neighbors will be. Are they aspiring jazz drummers? Opera singers? Do they work at night and sleep in the day? If the place does not feel right or seems like it will be a difficult place to get your work done, then move on to the next possibility.

If you absolutely have to have roommates, live with other law students—at least they will understand what you are going through. It can actually be quite helpful for a first-year law student to live with law students in their second and third years. The senior students often have good tips about professors, what to pay attention to in certain classes, and where to find useful information. In addition, senior students can help you connect with people and can give suggestions about summer employment and interviewing. Of course, the first-year student in this situation will have to put up with a certain amount of "rookie" treatment, but that is unavoidable.

Avoid living with people who party or talk a lot. Living with nonlaw graduate students is OK but by no means great. If you have the money, live by yourself the first year. The closer you are to school, the better. Certain things that did not annoy you before will begin to bug you in law school. Two more obvious and frequently encountered annoyances are lengthy commuting time and searching for a parking place. Your time is so impacted in law school that frittering away minutes driving back and forth and looking for a spot to park can cause upset that is way out of proportion to the actual inconvenience. On this score, make sure you know what times of the day are the worst to arrive on campus.

Become familiar with the arrangement of the law school. Especially become familiar with the library. Ask for a guide to the location of commonly used resources, and ask about any tours or orientations the library staff might give. Summer is a good time to ask library staff members for special help. Maintain a good relationship with the library staff members—they can be enormously helpful. Most students treat library staff members as their servants and rarely even know the names of staff members. Try to be someone who stands out to the staff in a positive way; they are a tremendous resource that goes largely untapped. Also, most head librarians at law schools are lawyers as well as professional librarians, and they usually like to help students with interesting research problems.

Figure out in advance where and when you will do your weekly shopping. Do not do your shopping during popular shopping hours; as with commuting and other time-wasting endeavors, you will just get upset. Shop late at night or early in the morning. Also, make sure that infrequent activities are taken care of before the semester begins. For example, if you wear glasses, make sure to get a full eye exam, and any new glasses prescribed, well before the semester begins. If you use prescription drugs, try to get several months' worth before you begin school.

Have a fund of several thousand dollars to carry you through the first few months of school. Often, financial aid disbursements are slow in coming. If you do not have cash, try to arrange something with relatives or apply for credit cards or a line of credit with a bank. You should have enough financial wherewithal to make it through a semester.

You should think of the telephone as the most dangerous device in your house or apartment.

Open your bank accounts and club memberships and get your gas, electricity, water, garbage, and telephone taken care of well before class starts. You should think of the telephone as the most dangerous device in your house or apartment. With old friends from home, new friends at law school, and relatives across the country, your telephone could be ringing off the wall and taking up your time in huge chunks. It may sound a bit antisocial, but schedule family and friend talk for a certain evening each week. Just put this information right in your phone message, and never pick up the phone when it rings—screen everything. When returning calls to classmates, do not make the mistake of getting into conversations beginning, "What about Professor X grilling Angela the other day?" Entering one of these conversations will probably entail a 30-minute struggle to get free.

Make a detailed weekly schedule for everything that you do. This includes exercise, movies, study time (allot 4 hours per day minimum), class-note entry, and television. Try to schedule as much homework time as possible during breaks between classes during the day. Too many students fritter the days away when they could be freeing up their evenings by studying for the next day's assignments at school. Schedule at least 1 hour for lunch, and try to always have lunch with classmates. Your class will probably be full of interesting people who have experiences that are very different from your own. Get to know these people, but decide early on who the people are in your class that you really like and want to spend time with. As for the rest, even the ones that you sort of like, do not commit any time to them. If you are already at a function you budgeted time for, such as a lunch or class party, by all means be gregarious, but do not schedule your leisure time activities with people you do not really want to be with. Time is too precious in law school. I sometimes tell people that you know you are in law school when you get mad at yourself for forgetting to take your contracts book with you when you go to the bathroom.

My last piece of introductory advice: try not to fall in love while you are in law school. If you do, you can kiss your schedule and orderly life good-bye. Alas, if you must fall in love, try to make sure you fall in love with another law student—at least that way you can study together.

THE BEGINNING

The first few weeks of law school are an anxiety-ridden, uncomfortable time, but they can be made easier if you understand what is going to happen in the first semester. Most schools have orientations for new students, but there seem to be mixed reviews about whether these orientations do much good or merely increase anxiety. As with anything else, this depends on how it is done and who is doing it. You should have a handle on what it is you will be doing and facing before you begin law school. You should find out as much as you can about how the school does things. You might also read some sources on law school education that can put you in the proper frame of mind. Two good sources are Scott Turow's *One L* and Karl Llewellyn's classic, *The Bramble Bush*.

The first year of law school is a disorienting experience, and it is meant to be that way. In law school, you do not so much learn law as you learn to speak and think like a lawyer; you learn the language of law. The type of logic and thinking that serves lawyers well is often very different from the patterns of thought students have acquired in their previous schooling. First-year law school often resembles and feels more like boot camp than like a purely intellectual endeavor. This analogy is apt in that law professors try to break down the presuppositions and pretensions of students and then build the entire class up together in a singular understanding of a legal subject or area. The important thing to remember is that almost everyone feels the same way you do—lost, somewhat depressed, a bit frightened, and wondering how they could ever have wanted to go to law school in the first place. You must never question your ability to succeed simply because you are temporarily off balance. Everyone in law school will have the same feeling.

Strange as it may sound, much of your potential in terms of job offers and other important opportunities is directly influenced by your first-year performance. First-year courses are mostly required of all students and provide a means of roughly sizing up the talent of an entire class. Probably more important, though, most of these first-year courses are in areas where the common law has ruled.

In courses such as torts, contracts, and property, the venerable tradition of the common lawyers is taught. Students are taught in these classes by learning how to parse dense case material into useable ideas or principles that may

> **First-year law school often resembles and feels more like boot camp than like a purely intellectual endeavor.**

then be applied to other cases or sets of facts. This is the traditional core of law school. There is a strong lingering belief that these courses represent the essence of legal training, and good or bad performance in these courses is often held to indicate whether or not someone is fit for the law. Anyone who thinks about this for a few seconds will realize how silly this assumption is. Nevertheless, the feeling that these common-law courses are the essence of law is still strong and, perhaps, even getting stronger. This is so for at least two reasons. First, these courses encompass tremendous amounts of Anglo-American legal history and have centuries of decisions and principles behind them. Second, because of this long history, it is taken for granted that the kind of reasoning required of the common lawyer—to glean from previous judicial decisions the principles behind them and the application of those principles to a current set of facts—is the epitome of how lawyers think.

From this rather small and provincial view of the essence of law comes much of the criteria for measuring the talent of law students. Make no mistake about it; your skill as a student and your estimated worth as a colleague are evaluated using the traditional markers of your performance in courses on common-law subjects. The primary means of introducing you to the common-law tradition are case reading and the Socratic Method.

THE SOCRATIC METHOD

Law professors generally introduce their students to common law through what is infamously known as the Socratic Method. Even in the hands of the most gentle practitioner, this method of instruction is very intimidating and can cause even self-confident students to question why they wanted to attend law school. The Socratic Method is considered by many to be a rite of passage, and any suggestion that we adopt more humane means of teaching are shouted down in good anti–Socratic Method fashion. In this method of teaching, the professor questions students about cases, statutes, rules, and so forth, thereby leading the student and the rest of the class to a greater understanding of the material than if they simply read an explanation or account of the matter. Sometimes, the questioning can be brutal, and the entire arrangement makes the student feel ill-at-ease. A student may be called on without notice and set to a 40- to 50-minute grilling that may begin with a seemingly unimportant case and end up far afield. Even now, I wither inside remembering some of the stupid things I said in front of a class of 140 people while being interrogated by a professor.

However, the Socratic Method imposes more serious costs than merely embarrassing and uncomfortable memories. It is highly intimidating and frequently reduces people to tears, anger, and humiliation. While not everyone is permanently disfigured by the Method, some people are scarred for life. Law students from groups that have been victimized by law and politics, including women and people of color, often see a much more substantial evil in this practice than do others. The law has traditionally ignored them, and when it did pay attention, it was often to engage in active suppression of their efforts to achieve equality. Members of these groups have often traditionally been rendered speechless, and these traditions continue to this day. For example, classroom studies show that women are far more likely to be interrupted, cut off, or scorned in classroom discussions. Professors, too, are far more likely to interrupt female respondents to questioning than male respondents. It is understandable then that many women and people of color are perhaps less than thrilled by the idea of a public grilling.

Many supporters of the Socratic Method see in it the reliable hand of tradition, but is it a tradition or pointless humiliation? I suppose I am in between these views. With the right professor, the method does not have to be humiliating, though it is unavoidably intimidating. Certainly, skill at formulating rational responses while under considerable pressure is a worthy talent to develop. Many students come out of this experience quite a bit tougher and quicker on their feet. As with anything else, the Socratic Method may be abused, and some professors no doubt wield it cruelly.

Despite controversy over its use, it is almost a certainty that you will suffer the Method in most of your first-year classes. Many professors let you know roughly when you can expect to be called upon. Take this as a challenge, and prepare as well as you can for the coming event. You probably will not know exactly which case you will be asked to give, so you must be prepared and know a number of cases very well. Study how the professor attacked student arguments and defenses in the past. Usually, professors have a few pet rhetorical and logical moves that can be discovered and prepared for. At first, these may be hard to dig out of the mass of detail in which they are enmeshed, but, if you look hard enough, these pet habits will soon reveal themselves. Prepare for these devices and perhaps even be brave enough to formulate a method of attacking them. While you must never be rude to your professor, it may be helpful at some

Law professors generally introduce their students to common law through what is infamously known as the Socratic Method. Even in the hands of the most gentle practitioner, this method of instruction is very intimidating and can cause even self-confident students to question why they wanted to attend law school.

point during a grilling to become a questioner, rather than just a victim. At selected points, a properly framed question may put the professor on the defensive momentarily. I say momentarily because you cannot hope to "win;" professors know this business very well.

CLASSES, STUDY GROUPS, AND STUDY AIDS

First-semester first-year courses usually meet approximately four times a week for an hour each time. Usually, these first-semester courses are torts, contracts, civil procedure, and criminal law or property. Along with these courses, you will be required to take legal writing, a course that meets only a couple of hours a week but is extremely valuable. Pay close attention to what your legal writing instructors say, and even though such courses are often pass/fail, put in as much effort as possible on the legal writing assignments. Researching is much of a lawyer's stock in trade, so make sure that you understand how to use all of the tools you will be exposed to in legal writing.

Students occasionally ask me if they should join a study group in their first year of law school. I always answer "yes," but that they should not rely on the group to do any of their work. It's OK to get involved in a group outline (a detailed digest of a course's material and concepts used to prepare for the final exam; some outlines can be quite lengthy) of your courses, but make sure that you do your own outline from your own notes, using the group outline to fill in any gaps and holes in your personal outline. Probably the most enjoyable times I had in law school came during these study sessions. Sometimes you sit with a study group and go through dozens of hypotheticals, twisting the facts slightly every few minutes to make the investigation remain fresh. These sessions can become quite intense as students near exam dates and can provide you with a great amount of insight into particular areas of the law.

Remember also that in law school, there usually are no midterm examinations or papers, at least not for first-year students. Your entire grade in torts, for instance, will probably hinge on a single 4-hour examination. The thought is really quite daunting by the time the end of November rolls around. After the hundreds of hours you have spent analyzing cases, principles, and the many areas of torts, your entire grade may hinge on what you can say about a fact pattern concerning liability for invitees on your property. Also, as you might surmise, the tests you get in law school are unlike any sort of test you have ever seen before. The tests are generally complicated "fact patterns" that you must analyze using what you have learned about various areas of law during your first semester. Many law schools have sections on their Web sites where past examinations are available. It certainly would not hurt to try to find and study back examinations by your current professors.

After the hundreds of hours you have spent analyzing cases, principles, and the many areas of torts, your entire grade may hinge on what you can say about a fact pattern concerning liability for invitees on your property.

In panicking over exams, students often purchase study guides for their classes. These guides are available from many publishers, but they all suffer from the fact that they cannot be specifically oriented to *your* classes. Each professor places significantly different emphases on areas of law than her colleagues, and a study guide necessarily must be over broad and likely will pay little attention to areas that you need to know the best. Nevertheless, I suggest that you go ahead and buy study guides to help fill in the gaps in your own outlines. In the first year, never depend on a commercial study guide as your main means of preparing for an exam. Buy the expansive, detailed outlines, not the cut-rate jobs. I was rather fond of Emanuel's line of outlines. Remember, though, that the emphases of your course will differ greatly from what is in the commercial outline since your instructor will tailor the course around her interests. There is no substitute for a good personal outline. Looking back on my grades, it stands out in high relief that the courses I got the best grades in were the ones in which I invested the time and effort to make a detailed, extensive outline from my course notes.

You should be rigorous in your schedule and have a reserved time for entering your class notes into your class outline. If you do not already have one, you should purchase a computer prior to law school. Spend the hour or so it will take each day to enter that day's notes into your personal outlines.

Finally, realize that you are going to be insufferable to your family during the holiday season after your first semester. Law will have become your life, but it will not have become the life of your relatives. As hard as it might be, try to avoid talking about law while you are home on vacation.

Law Schools and Contact Information

Appendix A

ALABAMA

Samford University, Cumberland School of Law
Birmingham, Alabama
Contact: Mitzi S. Davis, Assistant Dean for Admissions
Telephone: 205-870-2702
Fax: 205-870-2673
E-mail: msdavis@samford.edu
Web site: http://cumberland.samford.edu/

The University of Alabama School of Law
Tuscaloosa, Alabama
Contact: Betty McGinley, Admissions Coordinator
Telephone: 205-348-5440
Fax: 205-348-3917
E-mail: admissions@law.ua.edu
Web site: http://www.ua.edu/

ARIZONA

Arizona State University College of Law
Tempe, Arizona
Contact: Brenda Brock, Director of Admissions
Telephone: 480-965-6380
Web site: http://www.law.asu.edu/

The University of Arizona, James E. Rogers College of Law
Tucson, Arizona
Contact: Terry Sue Holpert, Assistant Dean for Admissions
Telephone: 520-621-3477
Fax: 520-621-9140
E-mail: holpert@nt.law.arizona.edu
Web site: http://www.law.arizona.edu/

ARKANSAS

University of Arkansas at Little Rock School of Law
Little Rock, Arkansas
Contact: Jean M. Probasco, Director of Admissions and Registrar
Telephone: 501-324-9904
Fax: 501-324-9433
Web site: http://www.ualr.edu/~lawschool/

University of Arkansas School of Law
Fayetteville, Arkansas
Contact: James K. Miller, Associate Dean for Students
Telephone: 501-575-3102
Web site: http://www.uark.edu/

CALIFORNIA

California Western School of Law
San Diego, California
Contact: Nancy C. Ramsayer, Assistant Dean for Admissions
Telephone: 619-525-1401
Fax: 619-685-2916
E-mail: admissions@cwsl.edu
Web site: http://www.cwsl.edu/

Chapman University School of Law
Orange, California
Contact: Office of Admissions
Telephone: 888-242-1913 (toll-free)
E-mail: jparamor@chapman.edu
Web site: http://www.chapman.edu/law/

Golden Gate University School of Law
San Francisco, California
Contact: Cherie Scricca, Assistant Dean of Admissions
Telephone: 415-442-6630
Fax: 415-442-6631
E-mail: lawadmit@ggu.edu
Web site: http://www.ggu.edu/law/

Loyola Marymount University, Loyola Law School
Los Angeles, California
Contact: Anton P. Mack, Assistant Dean for Admissions
Telephone: 213-736-1180
Fax: 213-736-6523
E-mail: admissions@lls.edu
Web site: http://www.lls.edu/

Pepperdine University School of Law
Malibu, California
Contact: Shannon Phillips, Director of Admissions
Telephone: 310-456-4631
Fax: 310-456-4266
E-mail: sphillip@pepperdine.edu
Web site: http://www.pepperdine.edu/

Santa Clara University School of Law
Santa Clara, California
Contact: Julia Yaffee, Director of Admissions
Telephone: 408-554-4800
Fax: 408-554-7897
Web site: http://www.scu.edu/law/

Southwestern University School of Law
Los Angeles, California
Contact: Anne Wilson, Director of Admissions
Telephone: 213-738-6717
Fax: 213-383-1688
E-mail: admissions@swlaw.edu
Web site: http://www.swlaw.edu/

Stanford University Law School
Stanford, California
Contact: Faye Deal, Director of Admissions
Telephone: 650-723-0302
Web site: http://lawschool.stanford.edu/

Thomas Jefferson School of Law
San Diego, California
Contact: Jennifer M. Keller, Assistant Dean of Admissions
and Records
Telephone: 619-297-9700
Fax: 619-294-4713
E-mail: jkeller@tjsl.edu
Web site: http://www.tjsl.edu/

University of California, Hastings College of the Law
San Francisco, California
Contact: Cornelius H. Darcy, Director of Admissions
Telephone: 415-565-4885
Fax: 415-565-4863
Web site: http://www.uchastings.edu/

University of California, Berkeley, School of Law
Berkeley, California
Contact: Office of Admissions
Telephone: 510-642-2274

Fax: 510-643-6222
E-mail: admissions@boalt.berkeley.edu
Web site: http://www.law.berkeley.edu/

University of California, Davis, School of Law
Davis, California
Contact: Sharon Pinkney, Director, Admissions
Telephone: 530-752-6477
Fax: 530-752-4704
E-mail: lawadmissions@ucdavis.edu
Web site: http://kinghall.ucdavis.edu/

University of California, Los Angeles, School of Law
Los Angles, California
Contact: Admissions Office
Telephone: 310-825-2080
Web site: http://www.ucla.edu/

University of the Pacific, McGeorge School of Law
Sacramento, California
Contact: Admissions Office
Telephone: 916-739-7105
Fax: 916-739-7134
E-mail: admissionsmcgeorge@uop.edu
Web site: http://www.mcgeorge.edu/

University of San Diego School of Law
San Diego, California
Contact: Carl Eging, Director of Admissions
Telephone: 619-260-4528
Web site: http://www.acusd.edu/

University of San Francisco School of Law
San Francisco, California
Contact: Saralynn T. Ferrara, Director of Admissions
Telephone: 415-422-6586
Web site: http://www.usfca.edu/law/

University of Southern California Law School
Los Angeles, California
Contact: Scott H. Bice
Telephone: 213-740-6473
Web site: http://www.usc.edu/law/

Western State University College of Law
Fullerton, California
Contact: Joel H. Goodman, Associate Dean
Telephone: 714-738-1000

Fax: 714-526-1062
E-mail: adm@wsulaw.edu
Web site: http://www.wsulaw.edu/

Whittier College, Whittier Law School
Costa Mesa, California
Contact: Alexis Boles, Director of Admissions
Telephone: 714-444-4141
Fax: 714-444-0250
E-mail: info@law.whittier.edu
Web site: http://www.law.whittier.edu/

COLORADO

University of Colorado at Boulder School of Law
Boulder, Colorado
Contact: Carol Nelson-Douglas, Director of Admissions
and Financial Aid
Telephone: 303-492-7203
Fax: 303-492-1200
E-mail: lawadmin@colorado.edu
Web site: http://www.colorado.edu/Law/

University of Denver College of Law
Denver, Colorado
Contact: Claudia Tomlin, Director of Admissions
Telephone: 303-871-6135
Fax: 303-871-6378
Web site: http://www.law.du.edu/

CONNECTICUT

Quinnipiac University School of Law
Hamden, Connecticut
Contact: John J. Noonan, Dean of Admissions
Telephone: 203-287-3400
Fax: 203-287-3339
E-mail: ladm@quinnipiac.edu
Web site: http://law.quinnipiac.edu/law.html

University of Connecticut School of Law
Hartford, Connecticut
Contact: Hugh C. Macgill

Telephone: 860-570-5127
Fax: 860-570-5128
E-mail: hmacgill@story.law.uconn.edu
Web site: http://www.law.uconn.edu/

Yale University, Yale Law School
New Haven, Connecticut
Contact: Jean Webb, Director of Admissions
Telephone: 203-432-4995
E-mail: admissions.law@yale.edu
Web site: http://www.law.yale.edu/

DISTRICT OF COLUMBIA

American University, Washington College of Law
Washington, D.C.
Contact: Sandra J. Oakman, Director of Admissions
Telephone: 202-274-4101
Fax: 202-274-4130
E-mail: admissions@wcl.american.edu
Web site: http://www.wcl.american.edu/

The Catholic University of America, Columbus School of Law
Washington, D.C.
Contact: George P. Braxton II, Director of Admissions
Telephone: 202-319-5151
Fax: 202-319-4498
E-mail: braxton@law.cua.edu
Web site: http://law.edu/

Georgetown University Law Center
Washington, D.C.
Contact: Andy Cornblatt, Assistant Dean for Admissions
Telephone: 202-662-9010
Fax: 202-662-9444
Web site: http://www.law.georgetown.edu/

The George Washington University Law School
Washington, D.C.
Contact: Robert V. Stanek, Assistant Dean of Admissions and Financial Aid
Telephone: 202-994-7230
Web site: http://www.law.gwu.edu/

Howard University School of Law
Washington, D.C.
Contact: Ruby Sherrod, Assistant Dean of Admission

Telephone: 202-806-8008
Fax: 202-806-8162
E-mail: rjsherrod@law.howard.edu
Web site: http://www.law.howard.edu/

University of the District of Columbia School of Law
Washington, D.C.
Contact: Vivian W. Canty, Director of Admission
Telephone: 202-274-7336
Fax: 202-274-5583
E-mail: vcanty@udc.edu
Web site: http://www.udc.edu/www/depts/law/welcome.html

FLORIDA

Florida State University College of Law
Tallahassee, Florida
Contact: Marie E. Capshew, Director of Admissions and Records
Telephone: 850-644-3787
Fax: 850-644-7284
E-mail: admissions@law.fsu.edu
Web site: http://www.law.fsu.edu/

Nova Southeastern University, Shepard Broad Law Center
Ft. Lauderdale, Florida
Contact: Nancy Kelly Sanguigni, Director of Admissions
Telephone: 954-262-6120
Fax: 954-262-3844
E-mail: sanguignin@nsu.law.nova.edu
Web site: http://www.nsulaw.nova.edu/

St. Thomas University School of Law
Miami, Florida
Contact: Peter Storandt, Director of Admissions
Telephone: 305-623-2310
Fax: 305-623-2357
E-mail: pstorand@law.stu.edu
Web site: http://www.stu.edu/lawschool/lawmain.htm

Stetson University College of Law
St. Petersburg, Florida
Contact: Jack Huebsch, Director of Admissions and Financial Aid
Telephone: 727-562-7802
E-mail: lawadmit@law.stetson.edu
Web site: http://www.law.stetson.edu/

University of Florida, Fredric G. Levin College of Law
Gainesville, Florida
Contact: J. Michael Patrick, Assistant Dean for Admissions
Telephone: 352-392-2087
Fax: 352-392-8727
E-mail: patrick@law.ufl.edu
Web site: http://www.law.ufl.edu/

University of Miami School of Law
Coral Gables, Florida
Contact: Therese Lambert, Director of Student Recruiting
Telephone: 305-284-6746
Fax: 305-284-3084
Web site: http://www.law.miami.edu/

GEORGIA

Emory University School of Law
Atlanta, Georgia
Contact: Lynell Cadray, Assistant Dean for Admissions
Telephone: 404-727-6801
Fax: 404-727-2477
E-mail: lcadray@law.emory.edu
Web site: http://www.emory.edu/

Georgia State University College of Law
Atlanta, Georgia
Contact: Cheryl Jackson, Director of Admissions
Telephone: 404-651-2048
Fax: 404-651-1244
E-mail: lawcry@gsusgi2.gsu.edu
Web site: http://law.gsu.edu/

Mercer University, Walter F. George School of Law
Macon, Georgia
Contact: Forrest Stanford, Assistant Dean of Admissions
and Financial Aid
Telephone: 912-301-2605
Fax: 912-301-2989
E-mail: stanford_fl@mercer.edu
Web site: http://www.law.mercer.edu/

University of Georgia School of Law
Athens, Georgia
Contact: Giles Kennedy, Director of Law Admissions
Telephone: 706-542-7060
Web site: http://www.lawsch.uga.edu/

HAWAII

**University of Hawaii at Manoa, William S. Richardson
School of Law**
Honolulu, Hawaii
Contact: Joanne K. Punu, Assistant Dean
Telephone: 808-956-7966
Fax: 808-956-6402
E-mail: lawadm@hawaii.edu
Web site: http://www.hawaii.edu/catalog/law.html

IDAHO

University of Idaho College of Law
Moscow, Idaho
Contact: John A. Miller
Telephone: 208-885-6422
Web site: http://www.uidaho.edu/law/

ILLINOIS

DePaul University College of Law
Chicago, Illinois
Contact: Dennis Shea, Director of Law Admissions
Telephone: 312-362-8013
Fax: 312-362-5280
E-mail: dshea@wppost.depaul.edu
Web site: http://www.law.depaul.edu/

**Illinois Institute of Technology, Chicago-Kent
College of Law**
Chicago, Illinois
Contact: Michael Burns, Assistant Dean
Telephone: 312-906-5020
E-mail: admitq@kentlaw.edu
Web site: http://www.kentlaw.edu/

John Marshall Law School
Chicago, Illinois
Contact: William B. Powers, Dean of Admission and
Student Affairs
Telephone: 312-987-1435
Fax: 312-427-5136
E-mail: 6alonzo@jmls.edu
Web site: http://www.jmls.edu/

Loyola University Chicago School of Law
Chicago, Illinois
Contact: Pamela A. Bloomquist, Director of Admissions
Telephone: 312-915-7170
Fax: 312-915-7906
E-mail: law-admissions@luc.edu
Web site: http://www.luc.edu/schools/law/

Northern Illinois University College of Law
DeKalb, Illinois
Contact: Judith L. Malen, Director of Admissions
and Financial Aid
Telephone: 815-753-1420
Web site: http://www.niu.edu/

Northwestern University Law School
Chicago, Illinois
Contact: Donald Rebstock, Assistant Dean for Admissions
and Financial Aid
Telephone: 312-503-8465
Fax: 312-503-0178
E-mail: nulawadm@harold.law.nwu.edu
Web site: http://www.law1.nwu.edu/

Southern Illinois University at Carbondale School of Law
Carbondale, Illinois
Contact: Patricia Caporale, Admissions Assistant
Telephone: 618-536-7711
Web site: http://www.siu.edu/~lawsch/

University of Chicago Law School
Chicago, Illinois
Contact: Richard Badger, Assistant Dean
Telephone: 773-702-9484
Web site: http://www.law.uchicago.edu/

University of Illinois at Urbana-Champaign College of Law
Champaign, Illinois
Contact: Pamela Coleman, Director of Admissions
Telephone: 217-244-6415
Web site: http://www.law.uiuc.edu/

INDIANA

Indiana University Bloomington, Indiana University
School of Law–Bloomington
Bloomington, Indiana

Contact: Frank Motley, Assistant Dean for Admissions
Telephone: 812-855-4765
Fax: 812-855-0555
E-mail: lawadmis@indiana.edu
Web site: http://www.law.indiana.edu/

**Indiana University–Purdue University at Indianapolis,
Indiana University School of Law–Indianapolis**
Indianapolis, Indiana
Contact: Angela M. Espada, Assistant Dean for Admissions
Telephone: 317-274-2459
Fax: 317-274-3955
E-mail: amespada@iupui.edu
Web site: http://www.iulaw.indy.indiana.edu/

University of Notre Dame Law School
Notre Dame, Indiana
Contact: Office of Admissions
Telephone: 219-631-6626
Fax: 219-631-6371
E-mail: law.bulletin.1@nd.edu
Web site: http://www.nd.edu/~ndlaw/

Valparaiso University School of Law
Valparaiso, Indiana
Contact: Heike Spahn, Director of Admissions and
Student Relations
Telephone: 219-465-7891
Fax: 219-465-7872
E-mail: heike.spahn@valpo.edu
Web site: http://www.valpo.edu/law/

IOWA

Drake University Law School
Des Moines, Iowa
Contact: J. Kara Blanchard, Director of Admission
and Financial Aid
Telephone: 800-44-DRAKE (toll-free)
Fax: 515-271-2530
E-mail: lawadmit@drake.edu
Web site: http://www.law.drake.edu/

The University of Iowa College of Law
Iowa City, Iowa
Contact: Camille de Jorna, Admissions Director

Telephone: 319-335-9095
Fax: 319-335-9019
E-mail: law-admissions@uiowa.edu
Web site: http://www.uiowa.edu/

KANSAS

University of Kansas School of Law
Lawrence, Kansas
Contact: Diane Lindeman, Director of Admissions
Telephone: 785-864-4378
Fax: 785-864-5054
E-mail: lindeman@law.wpo.ukans.edu
Web site: http://www.law.ukans.edu/

Washburn University of Topeka School of Law
Topeka, Kansas
Contact: Janet K. Kerr, Director of Admissions
Telephone: 785-231-1185
Fax: 785-232-8087
E-mail: zzkerr@washburn.edu
Web site: http://washburnlaw.edu/

KENTUCKY

**Northern Kentucky University, Salmon P. Chase
College of Law**
Highland Heights, Kentucky
Contact: Gina Bray, Admissions Specialist
Telephone: 606-572-5384
Web site: http://www.nku.edu/~chase/

University of Kentucky College of Law
Lexington, Kentucky
Contact: Drusilla V. Bakert, Associate Dean
Telephone: 606-257-1678
Fax: 606-323-1061
E-mail: dbakert@pop.uky.edu
Web site: http://www.uky.edu/Law/

University of Louisville, Louis D. Brandeis School of Law
Louisville, Kentucky
Contact: Glenda Jackson, Admissions Assistant

Telephone: 502-852-7390
Fax: 502-852-0862
E-mail: gjjack01@ulkyvm.louisville.edu
Web site: http://www.louisville.edu/brandeislaw/

LOUISIANA

**Louisiana State University and Agricultural and Mechanical
College, Paul M. Hebert Law Center**
Baton Rouge, Louisiana
Contact: Beth W. Loup, Director of Admissions
Telephone: 225-388-8646
Fax: 225-388-8646
E-mail: bloup@lsu.edu
Web site: http://www.law.lsu.edu/

Loyola University New Orleans School of Law
New Orleans, Louisiana
Contact: Michele Allison-Davis, Assistant Dean, Admissions
Telephone: 504-861-5577
Fax: 504-861-5772
E-mail: maldavis@loyno.edu
Web site: http://www.loyno.edu/

**Southern University and Agricultural and Mechanical
College, Southern University Law Center**
Baton Rouge, Louisiana
Contact: Velma Wilkerson, Coordinator of Admissions
Telephone: 504-771-5341
Fax: 504-771-2474
Web site: http://www.sus.edu/sulc/

Tulane University School of Law
New Orleans, Louisiana
Contact: Susan Krinsky, Associate Dean
Telephone: 504-865-5930
Web site: http://www.law.tulane.edu/

MAINE

University of Maine School of Law
Portland, Maine
Contact: Barbara Gauditz, Assistant Dean

Telephone: 207-780-4341
Fax: 207-780-4239
E-mail: gauditz@usm.maine.edu
Web site: http://www.law.usm.maine.edu/

MARYLAND

University of Baltimore School of Law
Baltimore, Maryland
Contact: Claire Valentine, Associate Director of Law Admissions
Telephone: 410-837-4459
Fax: 410-837-4450
E-mail: cvalentine@ubmail.ubalt.edu
Web site: http://lawschool.ubalt.edu/

University of Maryland School of Law
Baltimore, Maryland
Contact: Gary Wimbish, Director of Admissions
Telephone: 410-706-3492
Fax: 410-706-4045
Web site: http://www.umaryland.edu/

MASSACHUSETTS

Boston College Law School
Newton, Massachusetts
Contact: Elizabeth Rosselot, Director of Admissions
Telephone: 617-552-4350
Fax: 617-552-2917
Web site: http://www.bc.edu/lawschool/

Boston University School of Law
Boston, Massachusetts
Contact: Barbara J. Selmo, Director of Admissions
and Financial Aid
Telephone: 617-353-3100
E-mail: bulawadm@bu.edu
Web site: http://www.bu.edu/law/

Harvard University Law School
Cambridge, Massachusetts
Contact: Joyce Curll, Assistant Dean for Admissions
and Financial Aid

Telephone: 617-495-3109
E-mail: jdamiss@law.harvard.edu
Web site: http://www.law.harvard.edu/

New England School of Law
Boston, Massachusetts
Contact: Pamela Jorgensen, Director of Admissions
Telephone: 617-422-7210
Fax: 617-422-7200
E-mail: admit@admin.nesl.edu
Web site: http://www.nesl.edu/

Northeastern University School of Law
Boston, Massachusetts
Contact: Paul D. Bauer, Assistant Dean and Director of
Admissions
Telephone: 617-373-2395
Fax: 617-373-8865
E-mail: pbauer@nunet.neu.edu
Web site: http://www.slaw.neu.edu/

Suffolk University Law School
Boston, Massachusetts
Contact: Judge John Fenton Jr.
Telephone: 617-573-8155
Fax: 617-723-5109
Web site: http://www.suffolk.edu/

Western New England College School of Law
Springfield, Massachusetts
Contact: Eric J. Eden, Assistant Dean and Director of Admissions
Telephone: 413-782-1406
E-mail: eeden@wnec.edu
Web site: http://www.wnec.edu/

MICHIGAN

Detroit College of Law at Michigan State University
East Lansing, Michigan
Contact: Andrea Heatley, Assistant Dean of Admissions
Telephone: 517-432-0222
Fax: 517-432-0098
E-mail: heatleya@pilot.msu.edu
Web site: http://www.dcl.edu/

Thomas M. Cooley Law School
Lansing, Michigan
Contact: Stephanie Gregg, Director of Admissions

Telephone: 517-371-5140
Fax: 517-334-5718
E-mail: greggs@cooley.edu
Web site: http://www.cooley.edu/

University of Detroit Mercy School of Law
Detroit, Michigan
Contact: Joseph S. Daly, Assistant Dean
Telephone: 313-596-0200
Web site: http://www.udmercy.edu/

University of Michigan Law School
Ann Arbor, Michigan
Contact: Jeffrey Lehman
Telephone: 734-764-0514
Fax: 734-763-1055
E-mail: jlehman@umich.edu
Web site: http://www.umich.edu/

Wayne State University Law School
Detroit, Michigan
Contact: John Friedl, Director of Graduate Studies
Telephone: 313-577-3947
Fax: 313-577-1060
E-mail: jfriedl@cms.cc.wayne.edu
Web site: http://www.law.wayne.edu/

MINNESOTA

Hamline University School of Law
St. Paul, Minnesota
Contact: Theresa A. Decker, Director of Admissions
Telephone: 800-388-3688 (toll-free)
Fax: 651-523-3064
E-mail: tdecker@gw.hamline.edu
Web site: http://www.hamline.edu/

University of Minnesota, Twin Cities Campus, Law School
Minneapolis, Minnesota
Contact: Collins B. Byrd Jr., Director of Admissions
Telephone: 612-625-5005
Fax: 612-625-2011
Web site: http://www.law.umn.edu/

William Mitchell College of Law
St. Paul, Minnesota
Contact: James H. Brooks Jr., Dean of Students

Telephone: 651-290-6362
Fax: 651-290-6414
E-mail: admissions@wmitchell.edu
Web site: http://www.wmitchell.edu/

MISSISSIPPI

Mississippi College School of Law
Jackson, Mississippi
Contact: Patricia H. Evans, Director of Admissions
Telephone: 601-925-7150
E-mail: pevans@mc.edu
Web site: http://www.mc.edu/

University of Mississippi School of Law
University, Mississippi
Contact: Barbara Vinson, Coordinator of Admissions
Telephone: 601-232-7361
Web site: http://www.olemiss.edu/

MISSOURI

Saint Louis University School of Law
St. Louis, Missouri
Contact: Michael J. Kolnik, Director of Admissions
Telephone: 314-977-2800
E-mail: kolnikmj@slu.edu
Web site: http://www.slu.edu/

University of Missouri–Columbia School of Law
Columbia, Missouri
Contact: Sheryl Gregory, Director of Admissions
Telephone: 573-882-6042
Fax: 573-882-9265
E-mail: gregorysl@missouri.edu
Web site: http://www.missouri.edu/

University of Missouri–Kansas City School of Law
Kansas City, Missouri
Contact: Burnele Powell
Telephone: 816-99235-1672
Web site: http://www.law.umkc.edu/

Washington University School of Law
St. Louis, Missouri
Contact: Janet Bolin, Assistant Dean of Admissions
Telephone: 314-935-4525
Fax: 314-935-6959
E-mail: admiss@wulaw.wustl.edu
Web site: http://ls.wustl.edu/

MONTANA

The University of Montana–Missoula School of Law
Missoula, Montana
Contact: Heidi Fanslow, Admissions Office
Telephone: 406-243-2698
Fax: 403-243-2576
E-mail: hid314@selway.umt.edu
Web site: http://www.umt.edu/law/

NEBRASKA

Creighton University School of Law
Omaha, Nebraska
Contact: Maureen M. O'Connor, Assistant Dean
Telephone: 402-280-2872
Fax: 402-280-3161
Web site: http://www.creighton.edu/CULAW/

University of Nebraska–Lincoln College of Law
Lincoln, Nebraska
Contact: Glenda Pierce, Assistant Dean
Telephone: 402-472-2161
Fax: 402-472-5185
E-mail: lawadm@unlinfo.unl.edu
Web site: http://www.unl.edu/lawcoll/

NEW HAMPSHIRE

Franklin Pierce Law Center
Concord, New Hampshire
Contact: Lory Attalla, Acting Director of Admissions
Telephone: 603-228-9217
E-mail: lattalla@fplc.edu
Web site: http://www.fplc.edu/

NEW JERSEY

Rutgers The State University of New Jersey, Camden, School of Law
Camden, New Jersey
Contact: Camille Spinello Andrews, Associate Dean of
Enrollment, Law Admissions
Telephone: 856-225-6102
Fax: 856-225-6537
E-mail: csa@crab.rutgers.edu
Web site: http://www-camlaw.rutgers.edu/

Rutgers The State University of New Jersey, Newark, School of Law
Newark, New Jersey
Contact: Anita T. Walton, Director of Admissions
Telephone: 973-353-5557
Fax: 973-353-1445
E-mail: awalton@andromeda.rutgers.edu
Web site: http://info.rutgers.edu/RUSLN/rulnindx.html

Seton Hall University School of Law
Newark, New Jersey
Contact: Kenneth G. Stevenson, Dean of Admissions and
Financial Resource Management
Telephone: 973-642-8747
Fax: 973-642-8876
E-mail: admitme@shu.edu
Web site: http://www.shu.edu/law/

NEW MEXICO

University of New Mexico School of Law
Albuquerque, New Mexico
Contact: Susan Mitchell, Director of Admissions and
Financial Aid
Telephone: 505-277-0959
Fax: 505-277-9958
E-mail: mitchell@law.unm.edu
Web site: http://www.unmedu/~unmlaw/lawsch.html

NEW YORK

Albany Law School of Union University
Albany, New York
Contact: Dawn M. Chamberlaine, Assistant Dean of Admissions

and Financial Aid
Telephone: 518-445-2326
Fax: 518-445-2369
E-mail: admissions@mail.als.edu
Web site: http://www.als.edu/

Brooklyn Law School
Brooklyn, New York
Contact: Henry W. Haverstick III, Dean of Admissions
and Financial Aid
Telephone: 718-780-7906
Fax: 718-780-0395
E-mail: admitag@brooklaw.edu
Web site: http://www.brooklaw.edu/

City University of New York, Queens College, School of Law
Flushing, New York
Contact: William D. Perez, Director of Admissions
Telephone: 718-340-4210
Fax: 718-340-4372
E-mail: perez@maclaw.law.cuny.edu
Web site: http://www.law.cuny.edu/

Columbia University School of Law
New York, New York
Contact: James Milligan, Dean of Admissions
Telephone: 212-854-2674
Web site: http://www.law.columbia.edu/

Cornell University Professional Field of the Law School
Ithaca, New York
Contact: Richard D. Geiger, Dean of Admissions
Telephone: 607-255-5141
Fax: 607-255-7193
Web site: http://www.lawschool.cornell.edu/

Fordham University School of Law
New York, New York
Contact: Admissions Office
Telephone: 212-636-6810
Web site: http://www.fordham.edu/

Hofstra University School of Law
Hempstead, New York
Contact: Amy L. Engle, Assistant Dean for Admissions
Telephone: 516-463-5916

Fax: 516-463-6091
E-mail: lawaee@hofstra.edu
Web site: http://www.hofstra.edu/

New York Law School
New York, New York
Contact: Pamela McKenna, Director of Admissions
Telephone: 212-431-2888
Fax: 212-966-1522
E-mail: admissions@nyls.edu
Web site: http://www.nyls.edu/

New York University School of Law
New York, New York
Contact: Kenneth Kleinrock, Assistant Dean for Admissions
Telephone: 212-998-6060
Web site: http://www.law.nyu.edu/

Pace University School of Law
White Plains, New York
Contact: Angela M. D'Agostino, Assistant Dean and
Director of Admissions
Telephone: 914-422-4210
Fax: 914-422-4010
E-mail: adagostino@genesis.law.pace.edu
Web site: http://www.law.pace.edu/

St. John's University School of Law
Jamaica, New York
Contact: Gloria Rivera, Assistant Dean and Director of
Admissions
Telephone: 718-990-6592
Fax: 718-591-1855
E-mail: grivera@sjulaw.stjohns.edu
Web site: http://www.stjohns.edu/academics/law/

State University of New York at Buffalo School of Law
Buffalo, New York
Contact: Jack Cox
Telephone: 716-645-6233
Fax: 716-645-5940
Web site: http://www.buffalo.edu/law/

Syracuse University College of Law
Syracuse, New York
Contact: Patricia K. Golla, Director of Admissions
Telephone: 315-443-1962

Fax: 315-443-9568
E-mail: admissions@law.syr.edu
Web site: http://www.law.syr.edu/

Touro College, Jacob D. Fuchsberg Law Center
Huntington, New York
Contact: Office of Admissions
Telephone: 516-421-2244
Web site: http://www.tourolaw.edu/

Yeshiva University, Benjamin N. Cardozo School of Law
New York, New York
Contact: Robert L. Schwartz, Director of Admissions
Telephone: 212-790-0274
Fax: 212-790-0482
E-mail: lawinfo@ymail.yu.edu
Web site: http://www.yu.edu/cardozo

NORTH CAROLINA

Campbell University, Norman Adrian Wiggins School of Law
Buies Creek, North Carolina
Contact: Tom T. Lanier, Dean of Admissions
Telephone: 910-893-1754
Fax: 910-893-1780
E-mail: lanier@webster.campbell.edu
Web site: http://www.campbell.edu/

Duke University School of Law
Durham, North Carolina
Contact: Dennis J. Shields, Assistant Dean for Admissions
and Financial Aid
Telephone: 919-613-7020
Fax: 919-613-7257
E-mail: admissions@law.duke.edu
Web site: http://www.law.duke.edu/

North Carolina Central University School of Law
Durham, North Carolina
Contact: Adrienne Meddock, Acting Assistant Dean
Telephone: 919-560-5249
Web site: http://www.nccu.edu/

University of North Carolina at Chapel Hill School of Law
Chapel Hill, North Carolina
Contact: J. Elizabeth Furr, Assistant Dean of Admissions

Telephone: 919-962-5109
Fax: 919-962-1170
E-mail: law_admissions@unc.edu
Web site: http://www.law.unc.edu/

Wake Forest University School of Law
Winston-Salem, North Carolina
Contact: Melanie E. Nutt, Director of Admissions and
Financial Aid
Telephone: 336-758-5437
Fax: 336-758-4632
E-mail: admissions@law.wfu.edu
Web site: http://www.law.wfu.edu/

NORTH DAKOTA

University of North Dakota School of Law
Grand Forks, North Dakota
Contact: Linda Kohoutek, Admissions and Records Officer
Telephone: 701-777-2104
Fax: 701-777-2217
Web site: http://www.law.und.nodak.edu/

OHIO

Capital University Law School
Columbus, Ohio
Contact: Linda J. Mihely, Assistant Dean of Admissions and
Financial Aid
Telephone: 614-236-6310
Fax: 614-236-6972
E-mail: admissions@law.capital.edu
Web site: http://www.law.capital.edu/

Case Western Reserve University School of Law
Cleveland, Ohio
Contact: Barbara F. Andelman, Assistant Dean for Admissions and
Financial Aid
Telephone: 216-368-3600
Fax: 216-368-6144
E-mail: lawadmissions@po.cwru.edu
Web site: http://lawwww.cwru.edu/

Cleveland State University, Cleveland-Marshall College of Law
Cleveland, Ohio
Contact: Margaret McNally, Assistant Dean for Admissions
Telephone: 216-687-2304
Fax: 216-687-6881
Web site: http://www.law.csuohio.edu/

Ohio Northern University, Claude W. Pettit College of Law
Ada, Ohio
Contact: Grant W. Keener, Assistant Director of Law Admissions
Telephone: 419-772-2211
Fax: 419-772-1875
E-mail: g-keener@onu.edu
Web site: http://www.law.onu.edu/

The Ohio State University College of Law
Columbus, Ohio
Contact: Jennifer Beadnell, Office Associate
Telephone: 614-292-8810
Fax: 614-292-1492
E-mail: beadnell.2@osu.edu
Web site: http://www.osu.edu/law/

The University of Akron School of Law
Akron, Ohio
Contact: Lauri S. File, Director of Admissions
and Financial Assistance
Telephone: 330-972-7331
E-mail: lfile@uakron.edu
Web site: http://www.uakron.edu/law/

University of Cincinnati College of Law
Cincinnati, Ohio
Contact: Al Watson, Assistant Dean and Director of Admissions
Telephone: 513-556-0077
Fax: 513-556-2391
Web site: http://www.uc.edu/

University of Dayton School of Law
Dayton, Ohio
Contact: Charles Roboski, Assistant Dean and Director
of Admissions/Financial Aid
Telephone: 937-229-3555
Fax: 937-229-2469
E-mail: lawinfo@udayton.edu
Web site: http://www.udayton.edu/~law/

University of Toledo College of Law
Toledo, Ohio
Contact: Carol E. Frendt, Assistant Dean of Law Admissions
Telephone: 419-530-4131
Fax: 419-530-4345
E-mail: law0046@uoft01.utoledo.edu
Web site: http://www.utoledo.edu/law/

OKLAHOMA

Oklahoma City University School of Law
Oklahoma City, Oklahoma
Contact: Peter Storandt, Director of Law School Admissions
Telephone: 800-633-7242 (toll-free)
Fax: 405-521-5814
E-mail: pstorandt@lec.okcu.edu
Web site: http://www.okcu.edu/law/

University of Oklahoma College of Law
Norman, Oklahoma
Contact: Kathie Madden, Admissions and Recruitment Adviser
Telephone: 405-325-4728
Web site: http://www.law.ou.edu/

University of Tulsa College of Law
Tulsa, Oklahoma
Contact: Velda Staves, Director of Admissions
Telephone: 918-631-2709
E-mail: velda-staves@utulsa.edu
Web site: http://www.utulsa.edu/law/

OREGON

Lewis & Clark College, Northwestern School of Law
Portland, Oklahoma
Contact: Martha Spence
Telephone: 503-768-6634
Fax: 503-768-6671
E-mail: spence@lclark.edu
Web site: http://www.lclark.edu/LAW/

University of Oregon School of Law
Eugene, Oregon
Contact: Randi Schnechel

Telephone: 541-346-1810
Fax: 541-346-1564
E-mail: randisch@law.uoregon.edu
Web site: http://www.law.uoregon.edu/

Willamette University College of Law
Salem, Oregon
Contact: Lawrence Seno Jr., Director of Admission
Telephone: 503-370-6282
Fax: 503-370-6375
E-mail: law-admission@willamette.edu
Web site: http://www.willamette.edu/

PENNSYLVANIA

Duquesne University School of Law
Pittsburgh, Pennsylvania
Contact: Ronald J. Ricci, Dean of Admissions
Telephone: 412-396-6313
Fax: 412-396-6283
E-mail: ricci@duq.edu
Web site: http://www.duq.edu/law/

The Dickinson School of Law of Pennsylvania State University
Carlisle, Pennsylvania
Contact: Barbara W. Guillaume, Director, Law Admissions
Telephone: 717-240-5207
Fax: 717-243-4366
E-mail: dsladmit@psu.edu
Web site: http://www.dsl.edu/

Temple University School of Law
Philadelphia, Pennsylvania
Contact: Marylouise C. Esten, Assistant Dean for Admission, Financial Aid, and Student Affairs
Telephone: 800-560-1428 (toll-free)
Fax: 215-204-1185
E-mail: law@astro.ocis.temple.edu
Web site: http://www.temple.edu/lawschool/

University of Pennsylvania Law School
Philadelphia, Pennsylvania
Contact: Janice L. Austin, Assistant Dean of Admissions
Telephone: 215-898-7743
Web site: http://www.law.upenn.edu/

University of Pittsburgh School of Law
Pittsburgh, Pennsylvania
Contact: Fredi G. Miller, Assistant Dean
Telephone: 412-648-1414
Fax: 412-648-2647
E-mail: miller@law.pitt.edu
Web site: http://www.law.pitt.edu/

Villanova University School of Law
Villanova, Pennsylvania
Contact: David P. Pallozzi, Director of Admissions
Telephone: 610-519-7010
Web site: http://vls.law.vill.edu/

Widener University School of Law at Harrisburg
Harrisburg, Pennsylvania
Contact: Barbara L. Ayars, Assistant Dean of Admissions
Telephone: 302-477-2210
Fax: 302-477-2224
E-mail: barbara.l.ayars@law.widener.edu
Web site: http://www.widener.edu/law/law.html

PUERTO RICO

Inter American University of Puerto Rico, Metropolitan Campus, School of Law
San Juan, Puerto Rico
Contact: Julio Fontanet, Dean of Student Affairs
Telephone: 787-751-1912
Fax: 787-751-2975
E-mail: jfontane@inter.edu
Web site: http://www.inter.edu/law.html

Pontifical Catholic University of Puerto Rico School of Law
Ponce, Puerto Rico
Contact: Ana O. Bonilla, Director of Admissions
Telephone: 787-841-2000
Fax: 787-840-4295
Web site: http://www.pucpr.edu/

University of Puerto Rico, Río Piedras, School of Law
San Juan, Puerto Rico
Contact: Luis Mariano Villaronga, Associate Dean
Web site: http://upracd.upr.clu.edu:9090

RHODE ISLAND

Roger Williams University, Ralph R. Papitto School of Law
Bristol, Rhode Island
Contact: Christel L. Ertel, Acting Director of Admissions
Telephone: 401-254-4555
Fax: 401-254-4516
E-mail: admissions@rwulaw.rwu.edu
Web site: http://www.rwu.edu/law/

SOUTH CAROLINA

University of South Carolina School of Law
Columbia, South Carolina
Contact: John S. Benfield, Assistant Dean of Admissions
Telephone: 803-777-6606
Fax: 803-777-7751
Web site: http://www.law.sc.edu/

SOUTH DAKOTA

University of South Dakota School of Law
Vermillion, South Dakota
Contact: Jean Henriques, Admissions Officer/Registrar
Telephone: 605-677-5443
Fax: 605-677-5417
E-mail: request@jurist.law.usd.edu
Web site: http://www.usd.edu/law/

TENNESSEE

**The University of Memphis, Cecil C. Humphreys
School of Law**
Memphis, Tennessee
Contact: Sue Ann McClellan, Director of Law Admissions
and Recruitment
Telephone: 901-678-2073
Fax: 901-678-5210
E-mail: uofmlaw@profnet.law.memphis.edu
Web site: http://www.people.memphis.edu/~law/

The University of Tennessee, Knoxville, College of Law
Knoxville, Tennessee
Contact: Janet S. Hatcher, Admissions and Financial Aid Adviser
Telephone: 423-974-4131
Fax: 423-974-1572
E-mail: lawadmit@libra.law.utk.edu
Web site: http://www.law.utk.edu/

Vanderbilt University School of Law
Nashville, Tennessee
Contact: Anne M. Brandt, Assistant Dean of Admissions
Telephone: 615-322-6452
Web site: http://www.vanderbilt.edu/Law/

TEXAS

Baylor University School of Law
Waco, Texas
Contact: Becky Beck, Admissions Director
Telephone: 254-710-1911
Fax: 254-710-2316
E-mail: law_support@baylor.edu
Web site: http://law.baylor.edu/

South Texas College of Law
Houston, Texas
Contact: Alicia K. Cramer, Director of Admissions
Telephone: 713-646-1810
Fax: 713-646-2929
E-mail: acramer@stcl.edu
Web site: http://www.stcl.edu/

Southern Methodist University School of Law
Dallas, Texas
Contact: Lynn Bozalis, Assistant Dean for Admissions
Telephone: 214-768-2550
Fax: 214-768-2549
Web site: http://www.law.smu.edu/

St. Mary's University of San Antonio School of Law
San Antonio, Texas
Contact: Bill Piatt
Telephone: 210-436-3532
Web site: http://stmarylaw.stmarytx.edu/

**Texas Southern University, Thurgood Marshall
School of Law**
Houston, Texas

Contact: Cheryl Hanks Love, Director of Admissions
Telephone: 713-313-7115
Web site: http://www.tsulaw.edu/

Texas Tech University School of Law
Lubbock, Texas
Contact: W. Frank Newton
Telephone: 806-742-3793
Fax: 806-742-1629
Web site: http://www.law.ttu.edu/

Texas Wesleyan University School of Law
Fort Worth, Texas
Contact: Deborah Fathree, Associate Dean of Students
Telephone: 817-212-4040
Fax: 817-212-4002
E-mail: law_admissions@law.txwes.edu
Web site: http://www.law.txwes.edu/

University of Houston Law Center
Houston, Texas
Contact: Sondra Richardson, Assistant Dean for Admissions
Telephone: 713-743-2181
Web site: http://www.law.uh.edu/

The University of Texas at Austin School of Law
Austin, Texas
Contact: Shelli D. Soto, Assistant Dean for Admissions
Telephone: 512-471-8268
Fax: 512-471-6988
E-mail: ssoto@mail.law.utexas.edu
Web site: http://www.utexas.edu/law/

UTAH

Brigham Young University, J. Reuben Clark Law School
Provo, Utah
Contact: Lola Wilcock, Admissions Director
Telephone: 801-378-4277
Fax: 801-378-5897
E-mail: wilcockl@lawgate.byu.edu
Web site: http://www.byu.edu/

University of Utah College of Law
Salt Lake City, Utah
Contact: Reyes Aguilar, Associate Dean for Admission and

Financial Aid
Telephone: 801-581-7479
Fax: 801-581-6897
E-mail: aguilarr@law.utah.edu
Web site: http://www.utah.edu/

VERMONT

Vermont Law School
South Royalton, Vermont
Contact: Geoffrey R. Smith, Associate Dean for Admissions and Financial Aid
Telephone: 802-763-8303
Fax: 802-763-7071
E-mail: admiss@vermontlaw.edu
Web site: http://www.vermontlaw.edu/

VIRGINIA

College of William and Mary, Marshall-Wythe School of Law
Williamsburg, Virginia
Contact: Faye F. Shealy, Associate Dean for Admissions
Telephone: 757-221-3785
Fax: 757-221-3261
E-mail: ffshea@wm.edu
Web site: http://www.wm.edu/law/

George Mason University School of Law
Arlington, Virginia
Contact: Office of Admissions
Telephone: 703-993-8010
Web site: http://www.gmu.edu/departments/law/

Regent University School of Law
Virginia Beach, Virginia
Contact: Charles Roboski, Director of Law and Government Admissions
Telephone: 757-226-4119
Fax: 757-226-4595
E-mail: lawschool@regent.edu
Web site: http://www.regent.edu/acad/schlaw/

University of Richmond, School of Law
University of Richmond, Virginia
Contact: Michelle L. Rahman, Director of Admissions

Telephone: 804-289-8189
Fax: 804-287-6516
Web site: http://law.richmond.edu/

University of Virginia, School of Law
Charlottesville, Virginia
Contact: Albert R. Turnbull, Associate Dean
Telephone: 804-924-7351
Web site: http://www.law.virginia.edu/

Washington and Lee University School of Law
Lexington, Virginia
Contact: Susan Palmer, Assistant Dean
Telephone: 540-463-8503
Web site: http://www.wlu.edu/

WASHINGTON

Gonzaga University School of Law
Spokane, Washington
Contact: Sally S. Poutiatine, Assistant Dean
Telephone: 509-324-5532
Fax: 509-324-5710
E-mail: admissions@lawschool.gonzaga.edu
Web site: http://www.law.gonzaga.edu/

Seattle University School of Law
Tacoma, Washington
Contact: Carol Cochran, Acting Director of Admissions
Telephone: 253-591-2252
Fax: 253-591-6313
E-mail: lawadmis@seattle.edu
Web site: http://www.seattleu.edu/

University of Washington School of Law
Seattle, Washington
Contact: Sandra Madrid, Assistant Dean
Telephone: 206-543-0199
Fax: 206-543-5671
E-mail: smadrid@u.washington.edu
Web site: http://www.law.washington.edu/

WEST VIRGINIA

West Virginia University College of Law
Morgantown, West Virginia
Contact: Janet Long Armistead, Assistant Dean for Admissions

and Student Affairs
Telephone: 304-293-5304
Fax: 304-293-6891
Web site: http://www.wvu.edu/

WISCONSIN

Marquette University Law School
Milwaukee, Wisconsin
Contact: Edward A. Kawczynski, Assistant Dean for Admissions
Telephone: 414-288-6767
Fax: 414-288-0676
E-mail: edward.kawczynski@marquette.edu
Web site: http://www.marquette.edu/law/

University of Wisconsin–Madison Law School
Madison, Wisconsin
Contact: R. Alta Charo, Chair, Admissions Committee
Telephone: 608-262-5015
Web site: http://www.law.wisc.edu/

WYOMING

University of Wyoming College of Law
Laramie, Wyoming
Contact: Debra J. Madsen, Associate Dean
Telephone: 307-766-6416
E-mail: dmadsen@wyo.edu
Web site: http://www.uwyo.edu/law/law.htm

Excerpts from *Hopwood v. Texas*

The following are portions of the opinion in *Hopwood* v. *Texas*, 78 F3d 932 (5th Cir 1996). In this case, Cheryl Hopwood attacks the admission policy at the University of Texas School of Law for discriminating against white applicants to the law school. The case is edited so that only the material covering law school admission practices at the University of Texas is left. Whatever the political and legal importance of this case, it provides us with a nice insight into the admission practices at a major university. The court describes the practice in detail, and it is useful to you in understanding how law schools arrive at admission decisions. The method Texas used could be found at any law school, and it agrees with the sorts of things I have heard about admission processes at a number of other schools.

HOPWOOD V. TEXAS

March 18, 1996

Before SMITH, WIENER, and DeMOSS, Circuit Judges. JERRY E. SMITH, Circuit Judge: With the best of intentions, in order to increase the enrollment of certain favored classes of minority students, the University of Texas School of Law ("the law school") discriminates in favor of those applicants by giving substantial racial preferences in its admissions program. The beneficiaries of this system are blacks and Mexican Americans, to the detriment of whites and nonpreferred minorities. The question we decide today in No. 94-50664 is whether the Fourteenth Amendment permits the school to discriminate in this way.

We hold that it does not. * * *

I.

A.

The University of Texas School of Law is one of the nation's leading law schools, consistently ranking in the top twenty. See, e.g., America's Best Graduate Schools, *U.S. News & World Report* Mar. 20, 1995, at 84 (national survey ranking of seventeenth). Accordingly, admission to the law school is fiercely competitive, with over 4,000 applicants a year competing to be among the approximately 900 offered admission to achieve an entering class of about 500 students. Many of these applicants have some of the highest grades and test scores in the country.

Numbers are therefore paramount for admission. In the early 1990's, the law school largely based its initial admissions decisions upon an applicant's so-called Texas Index ("TI") number, a composite of undergraduate grade point average ("GPA") and Law School Aptitude Test ("LSAT") score. The law school used this number as a matter of administrative convenience in order to rank candidates and to predict, roughly, one's probability of success in law school. Moreover, the law school relied heavily upon such numbers to estimate the number of offers of admission it needed to make in order to fill its first-year class.

Of course, the law school did not rely upon numbers alone. The admissions office necessarily exercised judgment in interpreting the individual scores of applicants, taking into consideration factors such as the strength of a student's undergraduate education, the difficulty of his major, and significant trends in his own grades and the undergraduate grades at his respective college (such as grade inflation). Admissions personnel also considered what qualities each applicant might bring to his law school class. Thus, the law school could consider an applicant's background, life, experiences, and outlook. Not surprisingly, these hard-to-quantify factors were especially significant for marginal candidates.

Because of the large number of applicants and potential admissions factors, the TI's administrative usefulness was its ability to sort candidates. For the class entering in 1992—the admissions group at issue in this case—the law school placed the typical applicant in one of three categories according to his TI scores: "presumptive admit," "presumptive deny," or a middle "discretionary zone." An applicant's TI category determined how extensive a review his application would receive.

Most, but not all, applicants in the presumptive admit category received offers of admission with little review. Professor Stanley Johanson, the Chairman of the Admissions Committee, or Dean Laquita Hamilton, the Assistant Dean for Admissions, reviewed these files and downgraded only five to ten percent to the discretionary zone because of weaknesses in their applications, generally a non-competitive major or a weak undergraduate education.

Applicants in the presumptive denial category also received little consideration. Similarly, these files would be reviewed by one or two professors, who could upgrade them if they believed that the TI score did not adequately reflect potential to compete at the law school. Otherwise, the applicant was rejected.

Applications in the middle range were subjected to the most extensive scrutiny. For all applicants other than blacks and Mexican Americans, the files were bundled into stacks of thirty, which were given to admissions subcommittees consisting of three members of the full admissions committee. Each subcommittee member, in reviewing the thirty files, could cast a number of votes—typically from nine to eleven—among the thirty files. Subject to the chairman's veto, if a candidate received two or three votes, he received an offer; if he garnered one vote, he was put on the waiting list; those with no votes were denied admission.

Blacks and Mexican Americans were treated differently from other candidates, however. First, compared to whites and non-preferred minorities, the TI ranges that were used to place them into the three admissions categories were lowered to allow the law school to consider and admit more of them. In March 1992, for example, the presumptive TI admission score for resident whites and nonpreferred minorities was 199. Mexican Americans and blacks needed a TI of only 189 to be presumptively admitted. The difference in the presumptive-deny ranges is even more striking. The presumptive denial score for "nonminorities" was 192; the same score for blacks and Mexican Americans was 179.

While these cold numbers may speak little to those unfamiliar with the pool of applicants, the results demonstrate that the difference in the two ranges was dramatic. According to the law school, 1992 resident white applicants had a mean GPA of 3.53 and an LSAT of 164. Mexican Americans scored 3.27 and 158; blacks scored 3.25 and 157. The category of "other minority" achieved a 3.56 and 160.

These disparate standards greatly affected a candidate's chance of admission. For example, by March 1992, because the presumptive denial score for whites was a TI of 192 or lower, and the presumptive admit TI for minorities was 189 or higher, a minority candidate with a TI of 189 or above almost certainly would be admitted, even though his score was considerably below the level at which a white candidate almost certainly would be rejected. Out of the pool of resident applicants who fell within this range (189–192 inclusive), 100% of blacks and 90% of Mexican Americans, but only 6% of whites, were offered admission.

In addition to maintaining separate presumptive TI levels for minorities and whites, the law school ran a segregated application evaluation process. Upon receiving an application form the school color-coded it according to race. If a candidate failed to designate his race, he was presumed to be in a nonpreferential category. Thus, race, was always an overt part of the review of any applicant's file.

The law school reviewed minority candidates within the applicable discretionary range differently from whites. Instead of being evaluated and compared by one of the various discretionary zone subcommittees, black and Mexican American applicants' files were reviewed by a minority subcommittee of three, which would meet and discuss every minority candidate. Thus, each of these candidates' files could get extensive review and discussion. And while the minority subcommittee reported summaries of files to the admissions committee as a whole, the minority subcommittee's decisions were "virtually final." Finally, the law school maintained segregated waiting fists, dividing applicants by race and residence. Thus, even many of those minority applicants who were not admitted could be set aside in "minority-only" waiting lists. Such separate lists apparently helped the law school maintain a pool of potentially acceptable, but marginal, minority candidates.

B.

Cheryl Hopwood, Douglas Carvell, Kenneth Elliott, and David Rogers (the "plaintiffs") applied for admission to the 1992 entering law school class. All four were white residents of Texas and were rejected. The plaintiffs were considered as discretionary zone candidates. Hopwood, with a GPA of 3.8 and an LSAT of 39 (equivalent to a three-digit LSAT of 160), had a TI of 199, a score barely within the presumptive-admit category for resident whites, which was 199 and up. She was dropped into the discretionary zone for resident whites (193 to 198), however, because Johanson decided her educational background overstated the strength of her GPA. Carvell, Elliott, and Rogers had TI's of 197, at the top end of that discretionary zone. Their applications were reviewed by admissions subcommittees, and each received one or no vote. * * *

Sample Personal Statements

These sample personal statements are only meant to give you an idea of how to approach the problem of saying something coherent and intelligent about yourself that will be of use to law schools. Some of the following statements are longer than is normally advised, but the length rule can be broken when you have something to say, as do these applicants. These longer statements also provide more substance for you to draw ideas from when preparing your own personal account.

PERSONAL STATEMENT—EXAMPLE 1

I grew up the youngest in a family of five. My mother and father divorced when I was a few months old. My mother struggled to take care of five young children on her own. Because her parents died when she was a little girl, she never considered giving us up for adoption or to relatives. My natural father never kept in touch with us. He never helped my mother care for us and so I never knew him and have no recollection of him.

My mother tried her best to ensure we had a good family life by marrying twice after her divorce from my natural father, but neither man in her life served as a role model for my three older brothers. My brothers suffered the most from the breakup of my parents' marriage and my father's abandonment of his parental duties. All three have ruined their lives through drug abuse and crime. My oldest brother lives from day to day without any hope and with the constant internal battle against a drug addiction, which he often loses. My second oldest brother has been in and out of state mental institutions for over fifteen years. He is forty-two years old and is schizophrenic. My third oldest brother is somewhere in New York City and he doesn't want to be found. He calls my mother from time to time to let her know that he's alive.

I talk about my brothers first because even though they had problems growing up, they managed to protect and shelter me from their troubles. They made me believe in fairy tales and tried to shield me from the ugly reality of the world. It was because I lived a child's fairy tale life that I would later learn that fairy tales don't come true. I would learn to struggle, suffer, and survive.

When I was eighteen years old my mother moved away and left me in New York City with my friends to attend college. I guess my mother thought I would easily succeed and become the first college graduate in our family and I would easily learn to be responsible and independent. She must also have assumed that because I had never struggled for anything, I would be okay and I would doubtless succeed in becoming a lawyer. What I learned was that nothing was certain or guaranteed anymore. I moved constantly and trusted all the wrong people. I lost focus of my goals of finishing college and becoming a lawyer.

At the age of twenty-one I married a man who physically and mentally abused me. I thought he would take care of me just like my family did and protect me like my brothers had. He provided me with all the material things I desired and was used to getting. He convinced me to drop out of college and abandon my dream of being a lawyer. He convinced me to alienate my family and my friends, and to live the life he chose for me.

My experience with him taught me how to suffer. I did not understand his physical abuse, and did not know how to handle it. I was too ashamed to tell my family and too scared to leave. I was too scared to struggle on my own. I was scared that I would not make it on my own. I chose to suffer silently and alone because in the back of my mind I thought my situation might get better but deep in my heart I knew otherwise. Finally, I was forced by him to do exactly what I feared the most, to go out on my own and learn to struggle and suffer without him. He thought this would teach me just how good I had had it with him and that I would beg to come back to him. He was right at first, I did beg to come back. The best thing he ever did for me was to say "no." I was forced to learn to live on my own and for myself, no longer putting my needs on the shelf, no longer his friend, lover or wife. It was time for me to take control of my life.

Initially as I struggled and suffered I still looked for someone to take care of me, because I had not yet learned to survive on my own. When I saw a commercial for the Army, I decided that Uncle Sam would be my new provider and I would no longer have anything to worry about. As it was, I was already working seven days a week, two jobs around the clock, just to pay my bills. I thought this would be a break for me and would take away the stress and hardships. Quickly dispelling my delusions, the Army taught me to survive. I discovered a deep inner strength in me that would not let me give up. I had no other choice but to learn to do for myself and to help others. I learned there was humiliation in giving up and pride in succeeding. I learned to "just do it" with no questions asked and no hesitation involved. Do the job right the first time and you won't have to do it again was a valuable lesson learned and essential knowledge to have. In the Army I learned to be leader and to set the example for other soldiers by being placed in many leadership roles. In advanced institute training, I was the bay sergeant in charge of sixty-three young ladies. Through our teamwork and dedication for excellence, our bay won many awards and received many privileges for being the "Best Kept Area" in the company while under my supervision. I was so proud of what I had accomplished and my ability to encourage others to work together for a common goal. I won the respect of many young ladies and they had my mutual respect. In the summer of 1990 while in the Army, I was on orders to go to Saudi Arabia during operation Desert Storm. At first I was scared but I received so much love and support from my family and friends until I wanted to go and fight for my country and for those I loved dearly. I never ended up going to Saudi Arabia, but I was always ready to serve my country.

Today, I have three beautiful children from my second marriage whom I am raising. For them, I've learned to survive. From my struggles, I've learned what I don't want for them and what I believe they should know. From my suffering, I've learned how to protect them better than I was protected.

I am thirty-three years old and so far I have many accomplishments that will contribute to my ability to succeed at being a good lawyer. I have watched my brothers destroy their lives but never considered following in their footsteps, I have endured a terrible marriage and survived. I am a veteran of the U.S. Army and I am loyal. I survived through my struggles and suffering and I realized that becoming a lawyer would not only fulfill a dream, but also complete the person I am. I want to give back to the community through the practice of law and my experiences have grounded me and brought forth a determination that will not allow me to give up. I believe the practice of law involves integrity, endurance, discipline and loyalty. These qualities were always hidden somewhere in me, but surfaced through my struggles.

I've always believed if I accomplish all my goals I will be happy and I am determined to find out if this is true. I sometimes wish that I didn't have to struggle or suffer to reach happiness, but I know that there is so much more to me because I have "been there and done that." I wouldn't trade my life or any of my life experiences for anything in the world.

> I will probably struggle and suffer through
> law school/
> I will definitely survive to become justice's
> tool/
> So let my life like the lawyer be/
> To work for justice with dignity

PERSONAL STATEMENT—EXAMPLE 2

I am the only girl and middle child in a family of five siblings. As is common in Hispanic culture, my status was automatically placed below that of my brothers by virtue of my gender alone. Even as a teenager, I was not allowed to go out to movies alone with my friends; my younger brother was sent to keep an eye on me and report back to my mother. Needless to say, I was also not permitted to date in high school. At that time, without the social life afforded to other girls my age, I turned to academics.

Captivated by muckrakers, yellow journalism and the sheer power of the printed word, I discovered through journalism my love for writing. The idea of writing something that would get the attention of my teenage peers, or anyone for that matter, appealed to me. In one column I wrote about gang activity at my high school. I argued for tougher disciplinary measures for gang members and against ineffective administrative procedures in dealing with gangs. However, one did not disrespect gangs in the school paper and expect it to go unnoticed. While my advisor feared for my safety, he agreed to run the column anyway. The day it ran, I walked into school with my head held high and prepared for the worst, but it never came. Instead I got people talking; talking about changes. I had succeeded in what I had intended for my writing. My senior year I became a correspondent for the El Paso Herald Post and earned an internship for the summer after graduation. Although I served as more of a gopher than a writer, no task was too small. I loved the opportunity to hang around the news room and witness seasoned veterans at work.

When summer ended I was terrified at the prospect of starting college. My mother had greatly encouraged higher education for the boys, but not for me, despite my accomplishments. At the slightest hint of struggle that initial semester, my mother would tell me to quit; to just give up. Perhaps in her own odd way she was trying to anger me into sticking to my guns and getting the job done. Regardless of her intent, the lack of support was discouraging. My mother was uneducated as was her mother, and from a cultural standpoint I would have better served my family by getting married and leaving home than by burdening them with the expense of my college education.

My second semester I joined a sorority to be in the company of women whose mothers and grandmothers had been educated, thinking I would find the encouragement I was lacking at home. The biggest attraction for me of sorority life was the dedication to service work. I believed in our founders' commitment to campus and community service, and I was soon made the service chairperson. Suddenly I was hit with the realization that few do the work that many take credit for doing. Disappointed with my sisters' lack of commitment, I sought other outlets for service work. By becoming a volunteer at the UTEP Women's Resource Center, I began channeling my energy into such events as Take Back the Night, The Clothesline Project and World AIDS Day.

In 1994, as I approached the end of my second year of college, I was fully dedicated to my service work and my writing as a media liaison for projects at the Center. As finals approached my body was giving out. I had been ill throughout the semester and was mentally and physically exhausted; my body collapsed soon after from fatigue. I was relieved to learn I was not seriously ill, though it turned out that I was pregnant. A child was the last thing I wanted or needed in my life, and I had to make a decision. Despite objections by many of my peers, I made an informed decision to keep my pregnancy and try to forge ahead with my education.

Although earlier in the semester I had helped start a campus pro-choice organization, those same peers were reluctant to support my decision. So I turned to my sorority sisters. My pregnancy was an embarrassment to my sisters and alumna. I was told the situation would be better for everyone if I quietly left the sorority. While I was deeply hurt, I realized more important matters were at hand.

Beginning that fall, I was working full time and continuing both classes and service work. Twelve hour work days were the norm, so something had to give. I left school that fall believing that I would never return. In trying through education to fight a culture that limited women to being mothers and wives, I had failed by becoming the statistical unwed mother. I spent the next two years in the work force. Although I excelled in management, those challenges could not equate to those I had loved in academics. I needed to do more for my daughter and myself. In the summer of 1996, 1 walked off the job and back into the classroom.

Unlike the scared, sheltered girl fresh out of high school, I was now a single mother, a little older but far wiser. While I had longed for my mother's approval when I began college, I now had the admiration of my daughter. As her role model, I'm obligated not merely to teach her about responsibility but also to show her what is right through my actions. I have balanced academics, a child, a household, and a job (sometimes two jobs) every semester while continuing to have my writings published and making the best grades of my academic career. The decisions to keep my daughter and to raise her alone could have devastated my academic career, but instead they made me into a strong, dedicated, and balanced person.

Guidelines for Recommenders

GUIDELINES FOR FACULTY RECOMMENDERS

TO: Recommenders for students applying to law school

FROM: Law School Preparation Institute, UTEP

RE: Recommendations for law school

DATE: 29 July 1999

We are in no way trying to suggest what substantive evaluations you should make about a student. Rather, we are providing this information to let you know the sorts of things that law schools wish to know about candidates for admission. We do assume for purposes of this information sheet that you are writing a favorable letter for the candidate. Law schools much prefer specifics to general observations. For example, even the statement "Ms. Brown is one of the best students I have had in a long time" is not so useful to the candidate as "Ms. Brown wrote one of the two best papers I have ever received from a student on Shakespeare's *Macbeth*." General statements of worth are perhaps best used in summing up the candidate in the final paragraph.

1. **Analytical skills:**   If you have a basis for judgment explain the candidate's analytical abilities relative to other students similarly situated. If possible, use specific examples of problems, experiments, proofs,

papers, etc. where the candidate exhibited noteworthy skill. Relating anecdotes from private conversation with the candidate is perfectly fine. Discuss the candidate's grades in the classes she has had with you and give the reader some estimate of where those grades place the candidate in the universe of students you have had for the applicable courses.

2. **Communication skills:** Describe the candidate's ability to use language. Is the candidate articulate and persuasive? Are her papers well written and effective? How do you evaluate her writing relative to her peers? Is her vocabulary what one would expect for her education level? Does she speak up freely in class or discussion? Do her colleagues defer to her when she wishes to speak? Are her assignments presented in prescribed and neat fashion? A description of a particular event can be very effective in getting across the candidate's ability to use language. Temperament is also a feature that law schools are interested in knowing about.

3. **Mastery and commitment:** How well did the candidate master the material of the course(s) she took with you? Did she show the capacity to be a professional in your area of specialty? Is this the sort of person you would encourage to go to graduate school for training in your area? Did the candidate demonstrate a high level of commitment and motivation in mastering the material for your class(es)? If the candidate has an anomaly in the record that you know about, address it directly. For example, if the candidate has a 2.8 GPA but is in your eyes a much better student than that number indicates, then please say so. If the candidate tells you she has a 143

and is in the 28th percentile on the LSAT, you may wish to say whether or not this level of achievement squares with what you know about her.

4. **Integrity and personal characteristics:** If you are able to make such judgments, comment on the integrity and moral qualities of the candidate. For example, if you know the candidate donates time to local charities, is a Big Sister, or does other good works, feel free to include this information in your evaluation of the candidate's fitness for law study. If you know something about the candidate that appreciably sets her apart from her peers, then by all means include it in the letter. Finally, what kind of lawyer do you think this candidate will be and why do you think what you think?

GUIDELINES FOR EMPLOYER RECOMMENDERS

TO: Recommenders for students applying to law school
FROM: Law School Preparation Institute, UTEP
RE: Recommendations for law school
DATE: 29 July 1999

We are in no way trying to suggest what substantive evaluations you should make about a student. Rather, we are providing this information to let you know the sorts of things that law schools wish to know about candidates for admission.

1. **Honesty and integrity:** Did you find the candidate to be trustworthy and honest? Would you trust this candidate with responsibility greater than that

you would entrust to an average employee? Do any explicit incidents concerning the integrity or honesty of the candidate come to mind? If so, feel free to relate these incidences in you letter of recommendation.

2. **Punctuality and dependability:** Did the candidate show up for work on time and could you depend on the candidate to get critical jobs done?

3. **Supervision:** Did the candidate require constant supervision or could she be depended upon to do her work without prodding or continual oversight? Did the candidate produce a high quality product when she worked for you? If she worked with the public, was she well liked by customers and what sorts of comments were made about her by the people she waited on?

4. **Creativity and imagination:** Did the candidate come up with ideas or procedures to make the work place more effective? If so, give examples of how the candidate improved the work place.

5. **Communication skills:** How would you rate the candidates communication skills. Did she work easily and efficiently with other employees or the public. Was she required to submit written work as a part of her employment? If so, what was the quality of writing and analysis exhibited?

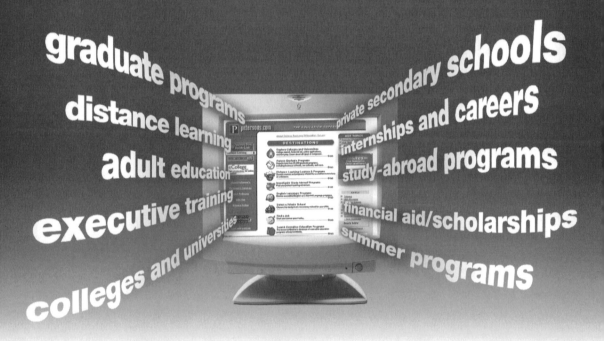